First published in 1994
Banff & Buchan District Council
Department of Leisure & Recreation

British Library Cataloguing in Publication Data

A catalogue record for this book is available from the British Library

ISBN 0 9522562 1 5

Printed by BPC-AUP Aberdeen Ltd.

'A STRANGER ON THE BARS'

The memoirs of
Christian Watt Marshall of Broadsea

edited by
Gavin Sutherland

designed and illustrated by
Dianne Sutherland

Published by kind permission of the Trustees of the late
Christian Watt Marshall

Banff and Buchan District Council
Department of Leisure and Recreation, 1994

"With the decline of the line-fishing and the rise of the herring industry, the women found themselves with less work to do at home and they too began to follow the herring. Leaving home in June they might remain in Shetland, Wick or the West Highlands till August. They would then pack up their kists and move to Fraserburgh, Peterhead or perhaps the Isle of Man. At the end of September they travelled south to Lowestoft or Yarmouth where they lived in lodgings until late Autumn. They remained at home during the winter months until the tour began again the following summer.

The Scottish gutting girl thus acquired a self assurance and knowledge of the outside world, rare in her contemporaries."

North East Scotland Library Service (NESLS), 1993

Christian, fourth from left, gutting herring at Dickson's Yard, Fraserburgh, c. 1917. Margaret, her sister, is next in line, and then Christian's life-long friend, 'Benjie's Kirsten'.

CONTENTS

ACKNOWLEDGEMENTS

Thanks are due to
The North East Scotland Library Service; Fraserburgh Heritage
Society; Suffolk Record Office; Yarmouth Maritime Museum;
George Gunn, Iain Macaulay, Anita Adams, Neal Murray,
Lorraine Noble, Robert Stephen, James Taylor, Barry Wain,
Paul Hamilton, Angus Mair, Helen Greig, Mike Rathbone,
and all at Network 90 Macduff for their kind and willing assistance
throughout the project.

ILLUSTRATIONS

"To my father and mother, and all who sacrificed their lives in the cause of freedom. Who so bears the whole heaviness of the wronged world's weight: why should their memory die?"

"No intelligent person can ever be ignorant if they keep their eyes and ears open, even though they have practically no education."
Christian Watt Marshall, 1985

FOREWORD

by
Lady Saltoun

To all who have read 'The Christian Watt Papers', these memoirs, written by her grand-daughter, will come as a welcome sequel. They overlap with those of Christian Watt, starting in the early 1900s in the fishing village of Broadsea, now engulfed by Fraserburgh on the north-east corner of Aberdeenshire, and she writes of many of the same people and their children. To those of you who read these but have not read Christian Watt, I would say that when you have read these, you should read Christian Watt and then read these again, because then you will get far more out of them.

The way of life Mrs Marshall describes changed very little from that of her grandmother's day until after the Second World War. It was hard, too hard, even bearing in mind the fact that both rich and poor had to put up with discomforts which we should now consider intolerable. But it was not unhappy. She writes of singing, both at work and during the journeys to the English fishing at Yarmouth; of music-making; singing and dancing after a day's gutting and packing herring in Shetland; and of dances and tea parties in the Broch. She had a lot of fun and laughter when she was young - perhaps more than people do today. But she also had more than her share of sorrow.

Mrs. Marshall's style is very similar to her grandmother's, as is her outlook on life, and her acute observation of the foibles of the human race. She has a great sense of humour, and no time for smugness, snobbery or pomposity. Her descriptions are vivid and she has an aptitude for that turn of phrase which "says it all". I particularly like her description of an obsessively clean and house-proud relative - "She cleaned for discomfort".

I strongly recommend this moving and evocative book, which I greatly enjoyed.

Lady Saltoun, May 1994

Broadsea Scholars
Christian, second row in white slip,
with her pals at Broadsea School, c. 1902.

Chapter 1
'THE SIXSOME CREW'

The sound of the sea was ever present in our lives. It was on our doorstep. In fierce gales waves came up to lick the walls of the Broadsea houses. We fell asleep and woke to the roar or the murmur of the sea. It was our living and the grave of many of our ancestors. Today we see rigs and oil traffic passing, and cargo ships with ore bound for the smelter at Invergordon. In my childhood the brown sails of a thousand fishing boats was a common sight in the Firth.

Three wifies working in Sandy McNab's fishhouse were all expecting at the same time. I was born at 72 Broadsea on March 26th 1896, the youngest of eleven children. Martha May, the wife of William Reid at 65 Broadsea, had a son Wattie who was a week older than me; he was eventually to be a veteran of the Battle of Jutland. Nellie McLean, the wife of Alex Crawford at number 75, had a son George, a month or two younger than us. Our mothers in the fish house had been nicknamed the "six some crew". We were all enrolled in Broadsea School on the same day.

I have memories of people talking about the Boer War but I didn't know what it was all about. In those days every housie was crammed with bairns, often with a different family in each end. The old folk were revered and respected. Many a far off aged relation ended his days in a half bed in the corner of somebody's kitchen. Some Broadsea houses had belonged to the same family for six generations or more.

My first day at school I cried when my mother left me. The teacher, Miss Pittendreigh, gave me two butter nuts. She lived to a great age and died in Grattan Place in the Broch. My next teacher was Miss Bella Noble, a Broadsea woman, then Miss Mary Hall and Miss Joy Milne from Pennan.

I was fortunate being the youngest in the family. I didn't have to suffer the poverty of the 1880s when folk were no more than galley slaves in every walk of working class life. By the time I came along, fishers were much better organised and many owned their own fishing boats and houses. From my youngest days, independence was dinned into me. I was told never to beg, borrow or steal, and to remember that the shilling in my pocket was my best friend. My father said, "We live in a practical world, not a world for dreamers. You must turn the thought into action."

When the herring season started, we watched sail boats passing, crowded with wifies and bairns lustily singing. They came down the Firth from Sutherland and Cromarty, and along the coast from Nairn and all the Banffshire places, with their pots and pans and bedding. Every wash house, garret and shed, and anywhere else a bed could be put up, was let. They came by the thousand and doubled the population of nearby Fraserburgh. At the end of May, the Broadsea School was so overcrowded that the school board took the Broadsea Hall for some of the bairns. The different accents were colourful. The "Achies", from Avoch on the Black Isle, never pronounced an H at the start of a word. I remember an Avoch loonie called Patience saying, "I 'eld out me 'and to get the strap!" We learned a lot from mixing with other folk.

During the fishing, the Lobbans from Rosehearty occupied the but end of our house. My father charged a shilling a week rent: it helped towards the rates. Our boys had to sleep in the loft above the box beds. It was the same in every cottage. It was amazing how everybody got by. Then, to be dirty or "throwither" was an unpardonable sin. Some fishers lived in their outhouses to keep the house nice!

In school, we had exams twice a year. When the inspectors came to examine our books we all sat like mummies. A lot of questions were asked, and heaven help you if you couldn't answer! An inspector once asked me to recite the

"Burial of Sir John Moore". I did it so well he gave me a brand new shilling! I thought I was rich, but was very down in the mouth when my mother handed it over to Meggie Mellis, the milk wifie who walked every day from a farm near the ruins of Inverallochy Castle with a yoke on her shoulders, carrying two large flagons of milk. My mother gave Meggie a cup of tea on a cold day.

Several of my mother's children died in infancy. Mary, my eldest sister, was a bonnie lass with fair hair. She contracted meningitis the night before she was due to leave for the Great Yarmouth fishing and died a day or two later. She was 19. I went with my mother to the Kirkton Churchyard a few days later - women didn't go to funerals then. I remember my mother cried bitterly. We wore black for a whole year.

I was terrified of both my parents. Bairns were seen and not heard. Parents didn't indulge their children with gifts and affection; they were chiefly concerned with earning a living. For us there was no childhood in the way folk think of it today. In fisher households we had to "buckle tee" and do our share of the work. We helped by mending herring nets, or redding and baiting lines. On leaving school, we had to find a job and contribute to the household economy. It was hard, but nevertheless we had a happy childhood.

I was at Broadsea School until I was 13. The Head Master was a Mr Broom, a cruel sadistic bully who took great pleasure in caning boys. He made them remove their trousers in his own room - it makes one wonder what his real motive was. One day, after dinner, Mary Cardno called at the door and said, "Kirsten, hae ye seen oor William? It's half past one and he has nae come hame for his denner!"

I told her Broom had given him a thrashing and locked him in the "black hole" under the gallery stair. Ink bottles were kept in this dreadful place and rats could be heard scraping behind the wainscoting. Poor William Cardno was two years younger than me. His mother went to investigate. A doorway led through from the school to the adjoining house where Donald's Mary's Margate, the school cleaner, lived. She blatantly refused to let the boy out and by two o'clock the whole Crawford clan had gathered to confront the Head Master. The poor child was sobbing in a state of hysteria, he had been in that place over two hours! Betty Milne, the granny, grabbed Broom by the tie and punched his face. She said, "I will strangle ye, ye ugly reed heidit bugger!"

Geordie Gunner's Nanse, the great granny, was a little wiry wifie. She gave the bully punch after punch below the belt, in the "delicate place", while Alex Crawford - Old Siddy - was getting a punch in here and there in his ribs. He kept on shouting, "Send for the police Miss Mary!" The whole class was hysterical with laughter. Broom got the hiding of his life! He strapped the whole class for laughing, but it was worth it!

Clothing was never bought off the peg. Lizzie Buchan made my Sunday clothes and my mother made the white slips we wore at school. At the "Little Wonder", which belonged to the Jacks of Peterhead but was taken over by Maitland, we could buy beautiful material at a reasonable cost. A man Duthie was the local agent for 'Singer'. He lived opposite Broadsea Hall. We bought a sewing machine from him, a great blessing to mothers. My mother often sat far into the early morning patching clothes or knitting so we could go to school looking respectable.

We played at "housies" among the rocks, with broken china from the dung middens along the west shore. Everybody had their own supply of potatoes planted at the nearby farms. Ours would be at "Roadside" or "Watermill" on the outskirts of the Broch. We did this right up to the Second World War. It was hard work for the wifies lifting tatties with a graip. By the time they were ready the men had all left for Yarmouth. We had a day off school to help our mothers - it's still called the "tattie holiday". In most houses the bags of tatties were stored under the kitchen bed and, by the time they were all used, they would be sprouting through the sacking. In the days before artificial fertilisers they tasted lovely.

Children gathered under the gas lamps, but we had always to be in early. Barbara Malley, who lived at 67 Broadsea, was a born comedian. She remained a lifelong friend. Joseph Noble, "Chappie", was a well off old widower who owned several houses. For a second wife he married a girl thirty years younger than him. He lived at 27, now 26 Broadsea. Late on the night of the wedding, after we thought they were in bed, Barbara Malley sang at their window, "I am only a bird in a gilded cage, a beautiful sight to see, I sold my love for an old man's gold, I am a bird in a gilded cage!"

At about the same time George "Sottie" Noble at

40½ Broadsea, now 16 Gaw Street, also married a second wife, a Gamrie widow who didn't know Barbara Malley from Adam. Barbara knocked on their door. "We are tinkie bairns from the Wasten," she said, "We hae had nothing to eat all day!"

The new Mrs Noble believed her and gave the whole jing bang of us a cheesecake each! Her children attended our school. One of them was Joe Watt, who later became the skipper of the *Gowanlea*. Joe won the VC in May 1917 when his boat was involved in action against an Austrian cruiser.

As a child, I was enrolled under the flag in the Salvation Army and went to the meetings every Sunday evening. We went to the Free Kirk Sunday School in Broadsea Hall, and we also supported the Parish Kirk meetings every second Sunday in Broadsea School. The other charge was Techmuiry School, where the alternate service was held. These meetings were conducted very sincerely by Mr Cadenhead, the Parish Minister's helper. He was a nice mannie. The Parish Minister was looked up to, but not his underpaid assistant, though he was a far better man. We noticed these things even though we were very young. My Granny went regularly, as did most of the old Bredsie folk. They sang 'The Lion of Judah shall break every chain', while under our breath we sang, "and Poshie the blacksmith will mend it again!" At one meeting, Jeannie McNab, a high spirited girl, cut the ostrich feathers from Donald's Mary's Margate's bonnet with a pair of scissors! "Margate," Jeannie said calmly, "the feathers on yer bonnet hae fan' aff!"

A Sunday School outing was always something to look forward to. The seats from Broadsea Hall were put on horse drawn lorries and a whole fleet went up the Court Road to Boyndlie, or sometimes to Philorth or Cortes. Great cartloads of bairns waved paper windmills and streamers. The weather always seemed to be scorching hot.

Every Sunday morning the Laird and his Lady, the

Ogilvy Forbes' from Boyndlie, came down the Court Road in a landau driven by two white horses, bound for the Catholic Chapel in the Broch. I remember the local doctor did his rounds in a pony and trap but such luxuries were few and far between. Lord Saltoun and his Irish Lady would often be seen in their carriage and pair. They used the Broadsea Post Office, especially during the fishing when the one at the Broch was busy. Today in the 1980s, I often see fishermen pass my door on horseback, sometimes with their children on a pony.

As a little girl, I enjoyed having tea with my mother as we sat by the fire mending my father's nets late at night. Everything was done within the house. We had a paraffin lamp and when the glass was newly cleaned it gave a wonderful light, but the slightest draught would alter the flame and blacken the glass. Our neighbours, Peter "Bainie" Wilson and Siddy at number 68, took in the gas with the same digging as us. It was something of a wonder to see the small black cast iron kettle boil so quickly on the gas ring. The gas bracket was low on the mantelpiece, and so handy for mending the nets which we stretched from a brass hook just below it.

In those days, folk wore themselves out with hard work. There was no old age pension or help of that kind. People depended on their families and most folk were too proud to ask for charity. Looking back, I see just how ill-divided the world was.

In my youth folk were more self-sufficient than they are today. We always prepared well for the winter. Every house had its own girnal of meal, half barrel of herring, kebback of cheese, bag of flour and two or three dozen stone jars of rhubarb and berries. The winter could come with its force twelve gales - we were secure inside our solid stone housie. With a cartel of peats and a ton of coal, we considered ourselves well off. Nobody was envious of anybody else - we were all poor but honest. At the shoppie, we had a jar filled with treacle direct from a barrel, the same with butter, and our dry stores. It was far better and much cheaper than all the prepacked stuff in supermarkets today - folk have to pay for all the wrapping now. Most of the shops then were kept scrupulously clean.

In a gale my father would stand guard at the door, and few would be allowed to enter. If a blast of wind did get in a huge section of tiled roof might lift. I often saw cottages tirred, it could happen so easily when the north gales blew.

It was a custom of fisher folk to visit friends and relations during the first couple of weeks of the New Year. A whole family might come to our house one night and we would give them a good tea with plenty of treats. Another night, we would go over to their house for supper. This went on until we had all visited each other. It was a very pleasant custom.

Our little house was built sometime in the 1600s and had changed little through the years. Like all the houses in Broadsea, it was a typical fisher's cottage with a large central closet and a box bed at each end. Near the kitchen fireplace the floor was laid with Caithness flagstones - the rest was beaten earth, freshly sanded every day. The but end had a wooden floor, plastered walls with a dado rail all round, and a varnished boarded ceiling. The ben had open rafter beams with boards laid across them to hold the fishing gear. The warmth of the house kept the nets and lines dry. The kitchen fireplace was an old hanging lum with a wooden canopy similar to a blacksmith's forge. Inside it there were tenter sticks for smoking fish and hams. Fishers sometimes kept a pig for curing, but that was before my time. Those wooden lums were dangerous brutes, they could catch fire so easily.

Nobody liked doing the small lines in winter. It was a messy job shelling mussels and baiting lines, but it was our living. The Wasten was as busy as Union Street in Aberdeen then. Folk had scaups all the way to the Millburn on the west side of the gut factory and wifies would be coming and going with lanterns in the dark. It was considered "Poverty Row" if a person used limpet bait to eke out their mussels on the hooks. We had to be careful - a lot of folk got blood poisoning by catching their fingers on the barbs of the hooks. It was hard and weary work with little reward. The drudgery was relentless. I have no knowledge of anyone in Broadsea who got Parish Relief, except maybe a few poor strangers who settled there.

Some women walked from the west end of Broadsea all the way to the Broch harbour with a baited line in a scull on top of their creel. It was about two miles there and back, and they usually came home with a creel full of fish. Sometimes they brought "haivels", large eels that could climb out of the creel and wrap themselves around your neck. Those things always gave me the jitters.

We called my mother's mother Granny Poll. She was Mary Johnstone and lived up the road at 55 Broadsea, now 45. Her husband, my grandfather, was James Taylor, known as "Bouff's Jimmy". He was lost at sea, leaving Granny Poll with a large young family to bring up. Her father, Peter Johnstone, was a Crovie man. Peter fought at Waterloo and died at 55 Broadsea at nearly 90 years of age. His wife was a Jane Third from Cairnbulg.

Granny Poll was a perfectionist, and very fussy. She was an excellent needle worker and made her living, even in old age, by hand sewing beautiful pillow cases and bed quilts for brides. She worked all the beautiful paisley patterns into plain cotton using designs of her own invention. Sometimes she mended my father's nets.

My granny had a good roomy house. The but was box plastered and the ben had a box bed with shutters that she always kept closed during the day. When people came in their thousands for the herring fishing, my granny let her

James Taylor, "Bouff's Jimmy", and Mary Johnstone,
Christian's 'Granny Poll'.

house to the same folk year after year. The Taylor brothers - William, James and Andrew - had a sail boat, and every summer three Highland men came from Lewis to make up the crew. Angus and Murdoch Mackinnon were brothers from Lochs near Stornoway. In the Summer of 1881 Murdoch became very ill and my granny, then a woman of 63, nursed him for ten days. During his illness he was visited regularly by Jeannie Noble, a Bredsie mission woman. He was 43 when he died and Jeannie spoke at his funeral. All the Highland folk attended the funeral, which was said at the door of number 55. His brother, a minister, led the service and they all sang in Gaelic. It was said about two thousand folk attended. Murdoch is buried in our ground in the Old Kirkyard.

I can just remember my aunt Jessie. She had an unhappy marriage. Her husband was the Chief Engineer on the Shetland Steamer *Queen*; he was a rotter and beat her constantly. Jessie, poor soul, liked a dram, but in the end she was converted in the Salvation Army. She died in Edinburgh at the early age of 42.

My uncle, George Taylor, was a thoroughly bad lot. His wife was a fine, hard working woman. She gutted with Lowe the curer all her working life. Uncle Andrew, known as "Heckie", and his wife had several children. They lived in my Granny's half house. Andrew was a good looking man with a great sense of humour.

George Street in Broadsea was opened when I was a little girl. Most of the houses were only finished to the first floor. The tops were left unplastered and completed as and when the owners could afford it. In the heyday of the herring, a lot of Banffshire folk settled in Broadsea. George Wood, who sat next to me at school, was a Cullen loon. His family later moved to King Edward Street in the Broch. Poor George was only 19 when he was torpedoed at Gallipoli - he was fished from the sea but later died of pneumonia. He was buried on one of the Greek islands near Rupert Brooke with the blue Aegean to lull him to sleep. I worked at the fish with Katrine Ann Hay, another Banffshire immigrant. A tinkie woman knocked on the Hay's door in George Street one cold winter morning. There was snow on the ground and the wifie's toes were through the auld bauchles on her feet. Katrine Ann's mother was a good Christian woman. I will never forget it. Without hesitation she took off her own shoes and gave them to the tinkie wifie.

I remember when a little tinker quinie died at the Wasten. Her funeral impressed us all. The cortège went past our door with hundreds of travelling folk in attendance. In the month of May the travellers gathered in great clans. They set up camp at Man's Haven, on the Broadsea side of the gut factory, where the well, known as "Mather's Wallie", kept them supplied with fresh spring water.

When I was really young, Mary McLeod and Magdalane Noble were my best chums. I often went with Mary to her aunt Jessie's house in College Bounds. Jessie was my mother's cousin. We used to visit her uncle Sandy Taylor and his wife Betsy at 50½ Broadsea. They were always very kind to us.

Granny Poll had a beautiful garden, where rose trees grew as high as the house. A large fuchsia grew by the back window and in the summer the smell of honeysuckle was overpowering. I'm glad that my cousin Jeannie and her husband are still living there. On the gable end of the house the fishermen built a shed for a poor wandering mannie called Ned Atkinson. He was an Englishman, one of the many who came North during the herring boom and later found themselves stranded without a home, and penniless. In a little outhouse at the back of Dunkie's Jeannie's lived another harmless wanderer we called "Convict Mackie". Keesie Bowman and his wife Buckie Bell also lived in an out house.

During the fishing, my grandfather's cousin, Billy Bounder, came in from Cairnbulg to live with my aunt Margaret, known as "Toodie", at 7 Broadsea. He was the village bellman and was very good at the fisher work. Margaret and her husband Alex Watt were very good to Billy. They also had a wifie, Mary Cadger, living in their shed. Alex later paid for her funeral. They had their own boat, *The Heather Bell*, and were considered quite well off by the Broadsea folk. My aunt was one of those women who cleaned for discomfort. We were never allowed to sit on the chairs - the place was spotless.

I was a delicate child and Granny Poll said I would, "never claw an auld heid" - I began this book when I was 83! I was always running errands for Granny Poll and the thanks I got was always the same, "Now run away and play".

Nobody had a spare penny in those days. The dallies in the yardie were starting to die-back, but before the first touch of frost they were lifted and stored under the bed. Granny was never to see those bonny "gollachy" flowers again. My brother Peter was in his bare feet and crying when

Granny Poll called us all to her bedside. I remember her telling us that soon she would be leaving. I can still see her now in her bed at 55 Broadsea, her head on a white frilled pillow. An old dresser stood by the bed with her blue plates, tureens and ashets on the top. Glass rollers hung on the wall near the snow white window screens, and Baltic bowls and Stafford figures were placed here and there around the room. Granny Poll was 87 when she died, closing another chapter in our lives.

Some nice shops came to the Broch in the early 1900s. I remember "The Maypole" and the "The Buttercup" opening up. On the day that Liptons opened, Mull's Mary rose at four in the morning and clung to the shop's front door to make sure she got the free whole ham Liptons had promised their first customer! Mary was a kind soul - she brought up a lot of waif children in her housie in the Waul

Park. The loons sailed their model boats in "Yowies Loch", a large pool next to Mary's housie. The land was drained a few years ago and a lot of new houses stand there now.

"Stoops" and his wife "Fittie Bell" lived at 75, now 82 Broadsea. Like all the old men in the village, Stoops wore a red flannel night cap all the time. Their eldest son was killed at Rorke's Drift in South Africa. Several Broadsea folk had settled in Footdee in Aberdeen in the early 1800s and Fittie Bell had relations there. She was a clean hard working wifie.

A piece of flickering soot on the grate bars or at the back of the fire bricks was said to herald the arrival of a stranger. One day my niece Maggie came to me and said, "Auntie Kirsten, there's a stranger on the bars!" The next day two nice university lads, one from Stirling and one from Sussex, came to my door asking about the fishing. I gave them a brief account as I remembered it. They suggested I should write a memoir.

Chapter 2
'BUFFALO BILL AND THE WIRELESS MAN'

As young girls, we often visited Jeannie Noble, an old spinster we knew as "Dunkie's Jeannie": the old house at 47 Broadsea has since been demolished. The older girls always took their knitting. I remember the interior of the house was ancient with a hanging lum. The wifie mended nets for a living but must have been quite well off at one time. The furniture was good, antique harp backed chairs with a deece to match, and drawers with old brass handles. She had a large kist with drawers in the bottom. It was always locked and she kept the key on a string around her neck. Many believed the kist was full of money! Jeannie took a stroke in her peat housie in the close one winter and was lying on the ground with snow on her face. Lizzie Taylor and Onty's Sandy carried her over to her brother's house where she died. In those days, people who took strokes never seemed to live more than a day or two, not like today when folk seem to have years of agony. Annie Buchan, Jeannie's niece, said to Lizzie Taylor, "You come with me as a witness, and I will take the key and open the kist."

It contained 9 gold sovereigns and some fine material given to her by the Saltouns, her regular visitors. Jeannie firmly claimed to be one of them. Only recently I discovered this was true, when I saw a birth register from Edinburgh that read, "James Gordon in Fraserburgh Castle had a son James born in Fornication." I can only say those aristocrats must have had a very different standard of morals for servant quinies than they had for their own sisters!

Broadsea School was said to be sinking but it's still there today, a fine dwelling house. A new school was built on Finlayson Street called the North School. It opened in 1909, and then stood in open country. The only thing near it was Marr's house and steading, now the Gospel Hall. Marr had about 15 acres around the school. Gamrie folk built houses on the opposite side just before the Great War. We met at the corner of Broadsea Road and, along with the pupils of the Penny Schoolie, we marched eight deep to the new Bredsie School. In our 13th year we were given leave of absence at the end of May to learn to gut herring. This I did with Mary McLeod and Mary Ann Cameron at Broadsea Farm with Willie Bruce. He was a nice man who never allowed the coopers to swear in our company. He stayed at Tillyduff House, across the road from the Broadsea Hall. We went back to school just before the end of summer term to finish the academic year.

We were sad to leave the old school. There had been a school on that site for centuries, but it seemed an eternity from August till Easter when we could leave at 14. I was only one year at the new school which still smelled strongly of new plaster and varnished pine. When Mr Broom took over the new school, the pupils of the old Penny Schoolie quickly learned what a tyrant he was. So much valuable time was wasted on useless stuff like the Wars of the Roses and Henry the Eighth's wives. Education then was tailored to make us as English as possible. They should have told us the history of our own country and the implications of the Industrial Revolution, and how it affected our own lives. In the final class, halfway up the girls' stair, our teacher was Miss Alice Brown. She later taught some of my own children. "Ma" Brown was an excellent teacher, but there was no hope of further education for any of us Bredsie bairns. At the age of 14 the entire class would go into domestic service, Maconochie's factory or to the fishing. A boy was lucky if he got an apprenticeship. All my brothers served for a trade.

Out of school and at home we spoke in our own Buchan dialect - a language quite incomprehensible to the English. The main aim of our education was, in fact, to stamp out our culture altogether. They taught us chivalry - girls bowed to teachers and the boys saluted them - but we knew it was a one-sided business. Broom would lift his hat to wifies he thought "society" but would pass a dozen Bredsie wifies without so much as a nod of the head! Wealthy curers were the same. Going into a shop they would beckon a lady to go in before them, but ordinary folk meant nothing. Curers would go to their yards and supervise 300 women who had been slaving from half past five on a Saturday morning until the Kirk bells rang for Sunday Morning Service! Thirty hours without a break for less than threepence a barrel!

There were a lot of poor folk in Broadsea. Jock Whyte and his wife Kirsten had a large family in the house next door. Kate McDonald and her husband, "Moleskin Jock", lived in an out house but their little home was spotless and her brasses always shone like dollars. All those bairns went to school with us, along with a horde of poor bairns from Broadsea Farm. The tinkies also attended our school - we knew them all well. My Mother told us never to scorn or snub anybody and always to ask the bairns to play with us. We never knew the meaning of snobbery.

From the age of nine our school holidays were spent in service looking after other folks' children. My first holiday job was with Willie Imlach, Miller Ritchie's foreman cooper, in the Barrasgate Road. There were four tenants in the house which, only a few years before, had been a classy fishcurer's residence. It had a proper bathroom on the first floor where we washed all the pots, a job I detested. My pal, Bella Noble, worked for Mrs Jamieson, the cabinet maker's wife, in the same house. One day she forgot to turn off a tap and flooded the place! Mrs May, young Jockie Borra's wife, was furious when the water ran into their part of the house! I slept in the garret with the two Imlach bairns who were not yet at school. They had a lodger in the front room, an insurance inspector called Morrison, who thought himself very grand.

I came down to the kitchen where Mr and Mrs Imlach slept one Sunday morning to help with breakfast. I carried a heavy tray of bacon sausage and egg through to Mr Morrison who was in bed with a poor raw country quinie. "Not a word about this," he said, "but bring another knife and fork through, and another cup."

Willie Imlach was still in bed when I went back to the kitchen and innocently told him that Mr Morrison had a girl in bed with him. Willie shot out of bed in his long woollen drawers and exploded into the front room. He flung Morrison's suitcase over the stair and he and his lady friend went after it just as quick. What a row! Willie was furious. "How dare you!" he said, "How dare you turn my home into a bawdy house!"

As Morrison ran down the stairs he pointed at me and growled under his breath, "I'll get you for this, you little bastard!"

Several years later my aunt Mary Jean was looking after old Annie Taylor, my grandfather's cousin. I was sent with Mary Jean's daughter, Elizabeth Ann, to fetch some kind of water bed from the district nurse in Sammy Robb's buildings in Grattan Place. When we rang the bell, who should answer the door but the erstwhile Mr Morrison. "It's you again you fisher bastard!" he screamed. We turned and bolted! Morrison chased us on to Victoria Street, but we could run in those days. By the time we got back, the poor wifie had died. I think those sort of men should be whipped! He had probably picked up the innocent child at the Broch Links and taken her in with his flash and glib tongue. Profumo, Jellicoe and Lambton, they were the same type. As for the Imlachs - they emigrated to Alaska. Their two young granddaughters recently paid me a visit.

I spent the following summer with my brother and his wife at 36 North Street. Barbara Buchan, "Barbara Caie" from Rosehearty, was keeping house for her younger brothers. They were staying at Miller's huts, while their mother was gutting and their father was at the herring. Another girl our age was Beldie McLeman, "Sally's Belle's Beldie", a Broadsea girl who was in service with Belle Burnett in the house next door to my brother's. Poor Beldie was used as a slave. We often gave her a hand, so the three of us could go up to the High Street to see all the ferlies. There was always plenty going on. Once we went to a Highland girl's wedding in Paterson's huts, the yard where the Co-op Supermarket now stands. We got tea and a fine piece. But Saturday night was best. The place was alive with Highland fishermen all speaking Gaelic, and there was plenty of Irish Gaelic too. We were forbidden to go to the Links Carnival. It was very popular and folk won good prizes, like clocks and tea sets. The Saturday market on the Broadgate was busy too, with lots of canvas stalls set up. Many local shop keepers kept a stall on the Broadgate, lit by naphta flares like the ones we used in the gutting yards.

Christian Noble was my school pal; she was always known as Bengie's Kirsten. We played with Jeannie Wattie, a quinie who lived with her granny, "Dookie's Jeannie", at 25 Broadsea. Dookie's Jeannie was a poor soul, but always very kind to us. After her granny died, Jeannie went to live with her two old spinster great aunts at number 19, Magdalene Noble and her sister Isa. On their dresser stood a jug with Sir Hector MacDonald's face on it. He was a crofter's son who rose to be a General in the army, hailed as a hero of the Boer War. We had a bowl with the General's picture on it - in fact you would find him in most houses in those days in some shape or form. I always remember old Magdalene Noble saying that he wasn't dead. She insisted that the General's suicide had been faked and that his coffin had been weighted with stones. Many thought that Sir Hector was now working for the Kaiser in Germany. Such stories were rife during the First World War.

At the end of the fishing, there was always a spate of Highland weddings in the herring girls' huts. Everybody turned out to see the bride and her maidens standing in their finery by the fireplace in the hut. All the bairns got a fine piece. When we were learning to gut with Willie Bruce, Kirsty MacDonald from Garyard wed a fisherman who crewed the *Rosevine* with my uncle Donald, "Donal' Brose". Mother sent me over to the hut with a pair of glass bread plates as a gift. We knew the man well. Mary McLeod, Bengie's Kirsten and I were given tea and cheesecakes in a hut at the corner of Park Street and the Braes. The bridegroom, Malcolm McLeod, was amused at Mary being a Broadsea Macleod.

I can't remember if it was the same minister, but at about the same time a Gaelic speaking minister, the Rev. MacDonald, was preaching in the Highland Kirkie. He had been connected in some way with the scandal of General Sir Hector MacDonald and, out of morbid curiosity, half the population of the Broch turned out to see the mannie. It was like getting in on a world event.

Fisher folk would never put shoes on the table. That was considered a terrible thing to do. They would never burn fish bones, even now I still adhere to this:

"Roast me, and toast me, but dinna burn my banes,
for I will lie a scarcity at your fire stanes!"

Then everybody had a tremendous respect for food. Even in the best of households it was often quite scarce. The herring season brought great crowds of folk to Broadsea. The fisher quines were always singing:

"Dinna think my bonnie lad I am fashed aboot ye,
Noo the fishin' time is here, I can dae withoot ye!"

Another old custom was getting "the cream of the wal". As the bells rang in the New Year, folk would be waiting to pounce and fill their bucket of water at the street well. If a wifie was beaten to it by a neighbour, they might not speak to each other for weeks! It was all so stupid.

A flagstaff was fixed at the head of Bruce's barrel store chimney, behind the Thomas Walker Hospital, and another rose high over the seaward gable at Gunther's buildings on the Castle Braes. When the sail boats were sighted, the watchmen rushed up ladders to the platforms below the poles and hoisted the Saltire Cross. This meant that the ships were laden with herring and signalled the women to the gutting yards. Betsy Borra from Inverallochy and Nellie May from Cairnbulg often came to my mother's house for tea. They were nice girls and they used to pleat my hair before I went to school. Nellie and Betsy were both living in Maggie Massie's garret at College Bounds. After a lifetime in Canada, Nellie came back to end her days in the Broch.

The great day came when Marconi the Italian wireless man arrived in Bredsie and the whole population of the Broch came to see him. It was a cold day and I remember he wore a fine fur coat. A mast had been erected in the field near Sottie's house in Gaw Street and Willie Malley was engaged as his watchman. Willie looked after the gear Marconi had stored in the half housie at number 67, the site now occupied by Cocky's house extension. Marconi was successful with his radio telegraphy and we were proud Broadsea had been chosen for the experiment. Long after that, his mast was used by the coastguard for breeches buoy practise. Some say that Marconi transmitted from Fraserburgh Castle, but that's quite untrue - he was never near Kinnaird Head.

I was eight years old when Buffalo Bill's Wild West Show came to the Broch. It was opened by William Cody himself. Besides all the animals and trappings, he brought a cast of 800 people across the Atlantic Ocean to the Broch

Links. The enormous staging was erected like a Western film set - houses and saloons with brightly painted verandas. It stretched from the Free Kirk on the North Links all the way to Kessock burn (the toolworks wasn't there then). Big Chief Sitting Bull and his Indians were fantastic. Annie Oakley was a crack shot - she was covered in medals. Everybody watched in wonder as she shot a cowboy's hat off. Above the silence we heard Babbie Johnnie's Bellie shouting, "Govey Dicks, ye will kill the chiel!"

BUFFALO BILL

AND HIS

INDIAN BRAVES

ON THE PIER AT FRASERBURGH.

Photographs of this Unique Event —
Whole Plate, mounted or unmounted, 2s each;
By Post, 2s 3d.
Cabinet, mounted or unmounted, 1s each;
By Post, 1s 1d.

Also a fine group of Indians on the Rocks at Kinnaird. Same prices.

These Photographs are Copyright and will be supplied by W. NORRIE only.

28 Cross Street, FRASERBURGH

Fraserburgh Herald, September 6th 1904.

William Norrie's souvenir photographs, 30th August 1904.

The like of Bill Cody's Show will never be seen in the Broch again. A lot of carnivals came to the Links in the years that followed. We thought they were great entertainment, but I suppose they would be too tame for this generation.

In September 1907, when the Master of Saltoun was 21, there was a big celebration bonfire on the links and all the school children were given an orange. The Bredsie folk, not to be outdone, flew the Yellow Lion on the hallie. The following week, the Master, dressed in his kilt, came to Broadsea School with his parents, the Lord and Lady Saltoun, and gave a short talk.

Miss Gladwell, a missionary, first appeared in the Broch that same year. She was a dedicated Christian, and so were her helpers - Miss Leech from Lancashire, Miss Morrow, an Irish woman, and a Miss Parkinson who went to Peterhead. Few could hold a candle to Miss Annie Gladwell's sincerity. Before Major Stewart, an ill-natured nasty sanitary inspector, pulled down all the houses in the old village, Miss Gladwell preached the Gospel on the little grassy square outside Betsy Noble's house, near Gunner's Wull's. She always had a good following at the Broadsea Hall too. I often went to hear her with my father and mother.

In the years preceding the First World War, Italian emigrants poured into Scotland to escape the poverty of Italy. Ice cream was new to us; we called it "hoci-poci". The Italians were in Lerwick and Stornoway and everywhere else. They worked hard and made their bairns work hard too. Peter Calligari was sea fowling at the Wasten when he accidentally shot a Broadsea woman scauping her mussels on the shore. There was a lot of laughter in the court when he said, "I aimed my gun at de mussel cockie, and shot de wifie on de dockie!"

A black man called "Ostrich Feathers" came round a lot. He sold good stuff but he could be quite impudent. My mother bought a beautiful pair of Satsuma vases from

Ostrich Feathers, and every house possessed at least one of his Japanese tea sets. Another salesman on foot was "Jimmy Bargains," a short, broad mannie with a large pack on his back. He bought direct from the mills.

Coming of Age Rejoicings at Philorth.

The Fraser Coat-of-Arms.

The Right Hon. Lord Saltoun.

The Right Hon. Lady Saltoun.

Majority of
The Master of Saltoun,

The Hon. The Master of Saltoun.

The Honourable
Alexander Arthur Fraser.

Gift from Fraserburgh.

Supplement to
"Fraserburgh Herald,"
10th September,
1907.

Philorth House.

In the season, we had Breton onion men. Several generations came, always on foot and with two long poles over their shoulders covered with strings of onions: the man who came to my mother came to me after I married. Supermarkets have put an end to all that trade.

My father had a terrible temper. I remember how my mother used to lie over the boys when he tried to hit them. He was as straight as a dye and stood for no nonsense. Our fishing boat, the *Venture*, was caught in heavy seas at the tail of the Hebrides when she turned turtle and a Highland crewman was drowned. My father swam supporting my twelve year old brother John as far as the Hysker Lighthouse. That episode practically took them both out at the door. His own father had been lost in the Phingask Bay, a tragedy that later put my Granny, Christian Watt, into the mental asylum at Cornhill. The old lady was a brilliant scholar and a great favourite with the medical students who helped her write her memoir. Without their help it would never have been done. She was a good needlewoman and produced beautiful work, even in her old age. For some reason she didn't like her own folk. She had a strange illness that only those who have encountered it could understand. Many scorned us for allowing the doctors to put her into Cornhill, but we had done all we could. When she came home it was all right for while, but then she would start feeding papers up the chimney in a desire for tidiness. It was impossible to sleep easy during her visits. Insanity is the price mankind has had to pay for an advanced civilisation.

I knew my mother's family better than my father's and mixed with them much more freely. The house at the corner of Gaw Street had originally belonged to Bouff's Jimmy's brother Alex, and number 62 belonged to his sister Isabella and her husband Jock McNab. Next to that was number 71, the home of another brother, Andrew. He was my friend Mary McLeod's grandfather. Everyone called him

The 'Venture', FR 984 in Fraserburgh harbour,
James Sim, "Brave" (a nickname he hated!), seated left.

"Onty". Bouff's family owned the whole row. A sister, Christian Taylor or "Bouff's Kitta", married a Watt at 66 Broadsea, and another brother, "Bouff's Jock" lived at number 29. I remember his wife Jane Noble, "Datty", standing at her door in a snow white mutch and striped petticoats. Matthew the slater was on her roof one day and I walked under his ladder. "Ye canna be a Taylor like yer mother," she said, "They are a' superstitious!" The Lobbans of Rosehearty, who lived in our house during the fishing, were grandchildren of Maggie Taylor, another sister in Pitullie.

Broadsea weddings were something besides. The betrothed couple called at every house in the village and every member of the family was invited to the reception at Broadsea Hall. In earlier years all the pans would be skirlin' as yellow haddocks were fried for the feast but later the local bakers cooked the fish, or steak pies when folk could afford them. Fishers have always had an obsession for beautiful china: we were often judged by the quality of our dinner sets.

The best would only be used on New Year's Day or at weddings. Marriage tables were really a show, with all the cakestands and polished cutlery. Coloured glass epergnes were filled with flowers and placed at every table. Some had five or six little glass baskets suspended from them, each one filled with sugared almonds and sweeties. In the afternoon, folk came up from the Broch to view the beautiful marriage tables. The newly married couple always led the dance in the grand march. There was no problem with drink then, it was all good clean fun.

When George Noble, "Sottie's Dodie", married Susan Strachan, I was ill and couldn't go to the wedding so I stayed with Granny Poll. I don't remember her name, but a wifie came to my granny's house wearing a beautiful lace edged tea apron. She brought a large basket of food and some sweeties - our share of the wedding feast. Granny laid the table with her best china and cutlery and the woman poured us tea from a polished brass kettle decked with ribbons. I was over the moon! Every old and infirm person in the village who couldn't attend the wedding got the same treatment. A different spirit exists today.

A dwarf wall and ornamental iron railing surrounded the hall in those days and old Danny McLeman, a girny character, was the caretaker. He lived at 78 Broadsea and was always good for a chase. We would sing, "Dare to be a Daniel, dare to stand alone, dare to hide at the back o' the door, and dare to throw a stone!" Bairns were never allowed near the hallie during his term of office. There was no vandalism in his day but today they have had to put wire netting on the windows. When Danny and his wife Lizzie fell out for a couple of weeks they would take an end each. When the but lum was reeking folk said, "That's Danny and Lizzie fan' oot again!"

Broadsea Temperance Walk took place on New Year's day. We had the Lodge Kinnaird, the Broch had

Lodge Faithlie and Pitullie the Lodge Craigullie. The Broadsea Flute Band led the walk to Rosehearty, followed by young and old folk alike. We marched through Broadsea before the Lodge Faithlie joined us for the walk to Sandhaven. There the Pitullie Lodge joined the ranks and we made for Rosehearty. In the square, often with snow underfoot, we had a short service and the band played a tune. The procession then made its way through the streets of Rosehearty and back onto the Fraserburgh road for the long walk home. We always got a special New Year's Day dinner: a hen with broth and dumplings followed by jelly and custard - a proper treat! The lovely smell in the village that day made our mouths water.

A soirée followed in the evening at Broadsea Hall. The same took place at the Templars' Hall in the Broch and the Schoolie in Pitullie. We hung up our stocking on Hogmanay Night - never Christmas Eve. We really looked forward to the morning when we would find our apples and oranges, and a sugar pig. The same had been a bairn's lot for a century or more. I often think that children today get far too much for their own good.

The Broadsea Temperance Flute Band, c. 1881.

It was the custom then to walk with your lover on New Year's Day. From about 1905, I took part in every walk and in the last few I had a partner. My first was Wattie Reid, and then Johnnie McLeman, "Tommy's Son", and then Andrew Lovie from the house where I now live. My last partner, on New Year's day 1914, was Boy Strachan from a house called "The Rest" in King Edward Street. I was not 18 until March and, although I was earning my own living at the herring, I had to get my father's permission to go to the conversashe in the Templars' Hall with Boy Strachan on 2nd January. At the walk we just joined arms with whoever happened to be there. A conversashe was an excellent form of entertainment. Small tables set with beautiful china and vases of flowers were arranged around the hall with a dance area in the centre. Folk drank tea, never spirits, and ate plenty of home bakes. I remember doing the Lancers to a fiddle and melodian. It was great fun. The urn was kept boiling and wifies were in attendance. It was there that the business of the Lodge was discussed. Most of the temperance folk were from the shore in the Broch, though some of the curers' daughters joined the movement, and Mrs Johnstone, the Congregational Minister's wife, was also a dedicated member. My escort had to have me home by 9.30pm. Boy's folk were all temperance. He was a fisherman and I remember being with him at Baltasound when the First World War broke out and the whole idea of civilisation collapsed around us. The entire band was slaughtered on the fields of Flanders.

In my childhood, only tinkie wifies smoked clay pipes. Even after the First World War it was considered distasteful for a woman to smoke. What awful lives those travellers must have had. For a long time I had no idea why they moved their camps a few yards every couple of days. I know now that it was the law. Police harassed them continuously. For all the hundreds of travelling folk who camped to the west of Broadsea, we never heard of anything ever being stolen. Before the Second World War the contractors of Broadsea Farm let the Waul Park to the travellers. They gave us a lot of fun on Friday and Saturday nights when they had all taken a dram! Even amongst those folk there was a strange kind of snobbery. A young woman used to come to our door to get her kettle boiled. She told me once how she had married below herself and how her husband, who was from "tent folk", had never set foot in a van before their wedding. They certainly seemed very happy despite their differences. She would always offer a penny for a hot kettle but we, of course, never took it. The blackout put an end to the travellers' way of life. They had to move into houses for the duration of the War and in time integrated with the community.

Our school janitor was Mr Smart but we called him "Tak A". He was was always chasing the truant loons, and my he could really run! Few got away from "Tak A". The Central School janitor lived with his wife and bairns at the top of the great clock tower. The climb up those stairs must have been hard work but the view I'm sure made it worthwhile.

When hired men came in from the country to crew the boats, it was tradition for skippers to provide their board. James Duncan, a poor country lad who came to work for Gilbert Noble, later went on to make a great fortune from the silver mines in Bolivia. James never forgot the kindness "Gibb" Noble and his wife had shown him and, when ever he was in Scotland, he paid them a visit. His motor car was the first I remember seeing in Broadsea. It was parked on the hairy hillock and all the town came to see it.

Chapter 3
'FROM HAIRY TATTIES TO HOLLYWOOD'

My eldest brother married Mary Milne six weeks after my sister Mary died. It was, needless to say, a very quiet affair. In 1905, my sister Jessie Ann married William Innes from St Monance in Fife. They had a big do in the Broadsea Hall and I was a bridesmaid. The night before the wedding was known as "feet washing night", when all the bride's presents were carried to her new home. That night the kitchen table was a real show with steak pies and rich food served to all those present, often a few dozen folk. The betrothed couple had to make themselves scarce for, if they were caught, they would get their faces and their feet blackened with boot polish. It made an awful mess of the house. I detested the custom, but it still happens today.

At wedding dances Ellen McLeman and Mary Noble, the hall cleaners, sold bags of scented conversation lozenges with messages like "You are my Heart Throb" on them. The young "romantics" bought them for their girlfriends; the bairns just threw them at each other.

In the May term, Mr Brown, the Estate Factor from Witch Hill House, came up to the hallie to collect a guinea for Lord Saltoun's ground rent. The whole village turned out on rent day. Ellen McLeman, who lived at 49 Broadsea, made the Factor's tea. She said, "Mr Brown told me they were the finest muffins that ever he seed!" For generations the McLemans had been known for their fine needlework, and Ellen was no exception. Her daughter made beautiful lace window screens.

My father brought home a little brown orphan lamb from Castlebay - no ewe would feed it. I called it "Ba Ba". It was such a darling, and knew all the bairns. My mother would take the dear little creature on her lap and feed it with a baby's bottle. It was tethered to the clothes pole with a collar like a doggie. I was heartbroken the day I came home from school to hear that somebody had stolen "Ba Ba". My father went to the police, but we never saw the lamb again. I'm sure my father would have killed the thief if he'd caught him!

The Taylors were a close knit family. Our neighbours were Bouff's Sanny's Jimmy, my mother's cousin, his wife, Kirsty from Gamrie, and their sons James and Alexander. One of the lads was an apprentice cooper, the other an apprentice rigger and sailmaker. After their father died, they were very poor. Apprentices were paid peanuts. My mother would put down the porridge pot to them after ours had been served. Number 73 Broadsea had been the home of my great grandparents Andrew "Bouff" Taylor and his wife Isabella May from Cairnbulg.

Alexander Taylor was one of the best. He died of tuberculosis when he was 19. My sister Jessie's son, Andrew Innes, was born on the day Alex died. When James Taylor was at death's door with pneumonia, his folk were sitting up all night with him. My sister had given his mother some wool to knit a pair of stockings. Another of my mother's cousins, Maggie Briggs, was sitting up with James one night when he suddenly looked up and said, "She's stolen Margate's wool."

Maggie said the poor thing was delirious, but he wasn't. Maggie had stuffed the wool into her shopping bag!

Maggie's husband was drowned in the 1881 Eyemouth disaster when the entire fishing fleet was lost in a freak gale. Another neighbour, Davie Maltman, lost his father on the same day. My daughter now lives in that house. It was rebuilt by my son, who now lives in Aberdeen.

My cousin, Elizabeth Watt, married a chap from Buckie and went out to Seattle. Her sister Jean married Willie Ireland from St Monance. I was at both their weddings. Willie's brother, Andrew, married Christina McLeod, Mary's sister.

Mrs Reid, "Martha May", was very good at cutting the boys' hair. She put a china bowl on their heads and cut around it. She made a neat job and the loons gathered a dozen at a time for a quick trim. When it was frosty, the kids filled buckets of water from the 'Pilot's Wal' across the road and poured it on the hallie pavement for a slide. When the older wifies put salt on it, we were most annoyed. We had no thought of old folk breaking their legs!

A crowd of us kids were sitting on Pilot's stair when Mrs Noble, "Isa Dallifer", the wifie from number 13, suddenly appeared. My pals all skedaddled, but she grabbed hold of me and gave me a few slaps around the lugs. Isa was most apologetic when she realised I was not her own daughter Beatrice! When she offered to explain it all to my mother, I told her not to bother. She would only have said that Isa hadn't hit me hard enough! Isa was from Whitehills. From that day on, she was always very nice to me. I still have good friends in Whitehills - Lena and her husband, Sam.

Mary Watt lived at 59 Broadsea with her daughter, Ellen Mackaskill. They were related to my father, and genuine friends of mine. Often on a Sunday they would ask me up to dinner; a plate of broth and a huge slice of dumpling. Long after, when I was gutting at Lowestoft, these people took me everywhere with them. They lived in the but end of number 59 and in the other end lived Mary's sister and her husband Geordie Cameron, a cooper, and their twin daughters Mary Ann and Magdalane. Geordie was a first cousin to Charlie Lowe in Strichen, the father of the celebrated Hollywood scriptwriter, Lorna Moon. Lorna regularly visited the Camerons at Broadsea, she was a very beautiful girl. Her real name was Nora Low. She died young in America, and her ashes were brought home and scattered on Mormond Hill. Everybody dried fish to make "hairy tatties", a delicious dish. I have seen Lorna Moon sit down and enjoy it before she became famous.

When Easter 1910 came along, a whole crowd of us left the school. We did not wait till July. Katrine Ann Hay (our camp boss), Chrisie Noble (Smoker's Leebie's daughter) and I got jobs with Davidson's, a Glasgow firm who rented premises in Gunther's yard on Denmark Street. Today it's a dull and dreary place. When the workers go home now, it's as silent as the grave but, when I first went to work there, it was bustling night and day. In those days, great crowds of herring girls from all over Scotland gathered in and around the Broch for the Summer season. Both sides of Denmark Street were lined with curing yards and herring girls' bothies. Today, most of the windows and doors are bricked up.

Since New Year, we had gone every Saturday to learn to fillet. To follow the fishing was our portion. So many good brains were wasted then. Though it was hard, cold work in the fish house, it was much better than looking after some other folk's bairns and scrubbing dirty porridge pots under a cold tap! We split the haddocks, and then washed and scrubbed them ready for the smoker's kiln. The fresh fish were packed in large boxes with ice and bracken, a plant which had some kind of preservative quality. We never grumbled. Unemployment was unheard of then - there were never enough people to fill the jobs available. The women were all kind to us. I remember a woman from the Shore, "Malley's Belle", helped us lift the heavy boxes. "Come my quinies," she would say, "and pit yer hands in this warm water". Chrisie Noble emigrated to the States with her entire family in 1912. She married a Highlandman, Angus Macaulay from Lewis, in Detroit. After 56 years away she came to stay with me for a holiday. We were life long friends.

I took "arles", an engagement fee of £2, to go to Baltasound to gut and pack herring for John Ewen and Sons. John Ewen and his sons were honest men. They were Baptists. I bought myself a pine kist when I signed up with them. It cost five shillings from Summers the cabinet maker in Albert Street. His shoppie is a hairdresser's now.

It was exciting to be going on the long voyage to Shetland. Two crews of girls were to share a hut. There were three girls in a crew, two gutters and a packer. My partners were Mary McLeod and Katrine Ann Hay; the other crew were Martha Taylor, Mary Jean Walker and Barbara Dingwall. In preparation for our eight or ten week stay, we each sent a small brown earthenware pig jar to the country to be filled with lovely butter. We took flour, sugar, tea, hard butter biscuits and other dry stores. We also took our bedding - we slept three to a bunk, one bed above the other with a glory hole at the side for buckets, basins and pots. A bonnie half tea set was packed along with a white table cloth, a velvet tablecloth, cutlery, dishes and a couple of rugs. During a weekend at Baltasound, it was nothing to make tea for three dozen relations.

All our goods and chattels were packed into herring barrels. The curers provided labels and had them loaded aboard the stock boat. Our gear would be waiting for us when we arrived at Shetland.

The SS St. Sunniva was berthed far down the breakwater. I was to sail several times on her before she was lost with all hands in an Arctic convoy during the battle of

"I think all the Broch came to see us off.
We were packed like herring in a barrel!"

the Atlantic. I think all the Broch came to see us off, my
mother among them. We were packed like herrings in a
barrel, with sheep and cattle for companions!

That day about 250 Irish girls and some men arrived
at Fraserburgh station. What a journey they must have had!
Many came from the West of Ireland, most from Donegal,
and they had already made one sea voyage and travelled the
length of Scotland by train. Some left home with a little food,
but many would have eaten nothing at all on their way here.
Margaret went to the station to meet the girls she knew.
They were all taken to somebody's home for a cup of tea, a
fried haddock and a wash. For years the same three came to
our house; Mary Laurie, Kate Murphy and Anna Cahill,
very nice Catholic girls. We were all ready to sail at six in
the evening, and with all on board the ship's horns blew and
the gangway was lifted. My first real adventure had begun.

The *St. Sunniva* had already been to pick up the
Peterhead folk - and what a crowd of girls! There were
sailings to Shetland every day that week. We ploughed

through the German Ocean abreast the sister ship *St. Ninian*. She had been to Buckie for the local girls and others from Banff, Macduff, Lossie, Nairn and the coastal villages. A third ship, the *St. Magnus*, had come from Leith with the girls from Fife and Eyemouth and others from Seahouses, Northumberland, Arbroath, Ferryden, Usan, Johnshaven and Gourdon. The Stonehaven, Fittie and Collieston girls joined the *St. Rognvald* at Aberdeen.

Fraserburgh Castle faded in the distance as we set our course through the Moray Firth. The thousands of Highland girls who, like the Irish, had already been travelling for some time, were picked up at Scrabster. The little port lay at the eastern entrance of the Pentland Firth and was handy for both Thurso and Wick. Though we were not allowed ashore on that voyage, I did manage to visit Scrabster many times in the years that followed. It was a busy place that reminded me of Rosehearty. The ship was jam packed with women but there were no life belts! There was no word of a life boat drill either, but at 14 we didn't think of such things; it was just good to be alive.

Kirkwall is dominated by St. Magnus Cathedral at the end of the main street. I noticed the narrow streets had gas lighting. We queued at the Castle Hotel for a cup of tea and a scone which cost three old pennies. We all bought a piece of crested china with Kirkwall's coat of arms on it. I still have the little Orcadian china housie I bought more than seventy years ago. It cost tuppence. When the steamer blew for all to come aboard three Broadsea girls had gone somewhere for a cup of tea and lost the ship. One of them sent a telegram to her mother - "Lost Boat". Her mother had everybody in Broadsea up to high doh: the word was that the ship had been lost! My mother went over to John Ewen's house to find out the truth.

Kirkwall was a pleasant break - it was a busy international seaport. In the open sea we saw a "skweel of muldoans" (a school of whales) and many porpoises. We called them "lowper dogs". These enormous fish can completely wreck a fleet of herring nets in five minutes. Going through the Roost, the stretch of water between Fair Isle and Sumburgh Head where the German Ocean meets the Atlantic, we were heaving and tossing and almost standing on our heads. Everybody spewed their guts! I lay on the deck thinking I was going to die. We were going through a "cross" sea, the wind blowing one way and the waves running in another. The smell of vomit was everywhere. We all vowed never to come back again, but in future years we all made the trip many times.

What a relief when Lerwick hove into sight. We passed the Knab and berthed at Victoria Pier. The hour ashore soon passed as we explored Commercial Street. It's a narrow, winding lane paved with flagstones and so crowded it's difficult to get through in places. With all its hustle and bustle the little street was nicknamed "The Roost". We bought candy in a little shoppie in a lane beside the graveyard. The wifie said, "Ye look awful pale my peerie lasses". She gave us a cup of tea, a God send after the sea sickness. We had been at sea for sixteen hours and were pretty well washed out. We thanked the wifie for her kindness and made our way back to the harbour. We boarded the steamer *Earl of Zetland* for the last leg of the journey up to Unst, Shetland's most northerly island. Today my son works on the oil rigs. He travels from Baltasound airport to Lerwick by bus.

Chapter 4
'ALCATRAZ'

We stepped ashore at Sandison's Pier in Baltasound and in no time we had our hut scrubbed and wallpapered: it was customary for the girls to take a few rolls of cheap wallpaper to cheer the huts up a bit. With a fire going in the brick fireplace and the kettle boiling, the place looked cosy. The huts were built like English back to back houses. At first floor level a long railed gallery ran the length of the wooden buildings on both sides and there was an open trap stair at each end. We were on the upper deck, looking towards Haroldswick. The rafter beams were not covered in and we could climb onto the joists and walk from one end to the other and see what everybody was doing. Fresh water was very scarce, but fortunately the rain showers were frequent and, with a water barrel at every door, we were never short of water to wash in. Drinking water was another matter. We had quite a way to walk for that.

With a nice bit of curtain net and a pair of curtains on the window, our hut was looking trig, and the crested china we bought in Kirkwall and Lerwick looked fine above the fireplace. I shared the top bunk with Mary and Katrine Ann.

The three stragglers who had been stranded at Kirkwall arrived the following day. Ailey Davidson, a Broch cooper, had stuck "Unclaimed Goods" labels on their backs! The poor quines must have wondered what all the laughter was about. When we started gutting we worked a long hard week under a lot of pressure. We were paid eightpence a barrel between the three of us. That's about three pence today! We lost a lot of sweat at the gutting, but the fun we had made it all worthwhile.

Baltasound was a busy place. There must have been about two thousand fishing boats there from the Broch and

Peterhead. The Broch curers were there in force. Bruce's had 300 women. Dickson, my sister Margaret's boss, had about the same and so did Eddie Gordon and James Farquhar Cardno. My boss, John Ewen, employed about 180 women. By 1910, there were great numbers of steam drifters at Balta and curers from every port in Scotland. Apart from the shallow half mile at the top, the girls' huts stretched the length of the loch on both sides. They even built on Balta Island which ran across the mouth of the loch. There were several curers there - Murison from Sandhaven, Gunn from Wick, Flett from Buckie, Buchan from Peterhead and Duthie from the Broch. I didn't know then that my future husband had served his apprenticeship as a cooper with Duthie in Castle Street in the Broch and as a loon he had worked on Balta Island; they called it "Alcatraz"! It must have been awful there, cut off from the stir ashore. It was a special treat for us to row over in Ewen's boat and have a sing song on the way. There was a well stocked shoppie in a wooden shed on the island, kept by a wifie who lived in a room at the back. She sold stamps and collected the mail, but it was franked at Baltasound. Her kettle was always boiling and the whole crowd of us would have tea and scones costing two old pennies. The store closed at the end of the fishing.

For us young quines, it was a great experience - the smoke from the drifters, the brown sails and bronzed fishermen, cargo boats and salt boats unloading, and flit boats ferrying goods and people around the loch. We would watch in wonder as the coal humfers nimbly walked across thin planks to coal the drifters. How they managed to cross from one wheel house to another with a hundred weight of coal on their backs I'll never know. For the Yarmouth humfers, coaling was even more dangerous. They had to cope with the constant flow of the river as well as the rising and falling tides. We were told that old worn shoes were the answer. They gripped the planks really well.

At Balta, there were pleasure yachts and ships flying the flags of more than twenty nations, and fishing boats from Norway, Denmark, Sweden and Holland. The Dutchmen wore their traditional trousers and wooden clogs and we would hear them clumping along the dirt roads when they came ashore.

There were hundreds of coopers at Balta and each station had its own cookhouse and cook. During the season, Sandison imported a lot of apprentice bakers from the mainland. They had to supply bread for twenty thousand folk! At home, the baker's apprentices were redundant when the greater part of the population moved up to Shetland, so their masters were happy to release them. Andrew Lovie, from 84 Broadsea was a baker at Balta, and so was John Noble from number 21. Nicol the Baker's son was drowned at Balta when his cobble capsized.

Sandison had a roaring business at the head of the loch with a pub adjoining the large General Merchant's Store. It was called 'The Red Flag'. The Post Office was open till ten at night for telegrams for the fish trade, and we posted cards every week. To save money we put a few in with each of our letters home.

When I started to work at the herring it was the end of the Edwardian era, but in actual fact that way of life went on until the First World War. Many of the fishcurers' children belonged to the group we called "the idle rich". They had no interest in town councils or anything like that, and scarcely gave their parents a glance. For them the money came rolling in, and we were the asses who provided it. They didn't work - that would have been unthinkable. So, while the curers' sons pursued life's pleasures, their daughters did nothing at all! This applied to the really wealthy curers - there were only a handful in that bracket. Many were comfortable and lived in the residential areas of the Broch, but they didn't belong to the "elite".

Today, there are people with money who put on a show and try to impress folk (with little success) but, before the First World War, it really had to be seen to be believed! In the north of Shetland, where the summer sun never sets, the private yachts that came into Baltasound were a wonder to look at. By the time we started to gut, at six o'clock in the morning, the sailors on the yachts were up and about. As they scrubbed the teak decks, the ships' cooks polished the brasswork till it shone like a dollar in the morning sun. Even the capstans were polished brass. The mahogany doors and casings were cleaned every day by crewmen who, like us, were working for nothing, while the owners lay in their bunks until eleven o'clock in the day. It was a decadent system, and so grossly unjust. Some of the curers had huts lined in for their wives and children - a lot of wet blankets who had made a fortune from other folks sweat! In the school we sang "Rule Brittania, Britons never never shall be slaves." By the age of 14 I realised just how untrue the song was.

All through the school we had been taught to respect our "betters", but my father would not allow us to read the trashy periodicals that supported that notion. Instead, he had us join the library and read sensible books. I have been a member most of my life; so was my pal Kirsten. Father wrote out lists of books for me to look out for. He wouldn't allow me to read fiction. Books in the real radical tradition were in very short supply in the days when libraries tended to cater more for the better off.

All over Balta, we could hear the sound of young feet flying up and down wooden stairs and running along the huts' galleries. Everybody was always in a hurry. Sandy Wood of Peterhead had the outermost station on the north side, near the entrance to the loch. The Peterhead girls were very jolly. Jeannie Ann Geddes, Mary Strachan and Ellen Buchan were our neighbours. Our station was next to

Wood's, and then there was Watt from the Broch and Sutherland from Wick. He had a cheerful crowd of girls who always sang late into the night. Then there was McKenzie, the Stornoway curer. He employed a few Broch women but most of his crews were Highland girls who sang in Gaelic. I think Stephen from Boddam was next to McKenzie. When our coopers went past Stephen's station they always shouted "Fa hangit the monkey?" We used to sing:

> *"There was a ship cam roon the coast,*
> *Sadly a' the crew wis lost,*
> *Except the monkey up the post,*
> *The Boddamers hangit the monkey oh!"*

Next to the Boddamers, there was Eddie Gordon. He had a big station employing girls from all over Scotland and some married women from Balta itself. Sottie Noble's station was in front of the ruins of Hamar House, a popular place with the courting couples. The old house must have been very grand in its day, surrounded by walled in kailyards and gardens. Little remained of the stables and outbuildings. Old Sottie couldn't read or write, but was a pleasant mannie and built up a good business that is still going. If he met us wandering about he would say, "You Bredsie deuks should be in your beds at this time o' nicht!" We had a lot of fun with girls from Noble's huts who were nearly all from Broadsea.

The south side belonged to the big curers. Downie was directly opposite us and Paterson's station was next to the gut factory. Curiously, the gut factory didn't smell like the one in the Broch today. Then the guts were processed fresh from the sea; the herring didn't lie frozen for two weeks in the hold of a drifter. My friend, Bengie's Kirsten, was on the south side with Dickson. My sister Margaret had agreed to take her with her as a learner.

At every Balta fishing the naval warship *HMS Ringdove*

came to police the loch. Before we left home, my father forbade us to look at the sailors who came ashore at weekends. He always gave us a great list of do's and don'ts before we left for Balta. We gave a cup of tea to the fishing boat's cook loonies when ever we got the chance - they had a hard job coiling the tarry leader ropes. They were known as "coiler" and "the kettle boiler". Their hands, like ours, were often just raw flesh. A Church of Scotland dressing station operated on the south side and The Faith Mission had another to the north.

The herring fleet in Baltasound.
John Ewen's curing yard is on the right.

Herring came in by the thousand cran. It was hard work lifting heavy wooden tubs from six in the morning sometimes until two next morning. Many girls aimed to be the number one crew, the crew that filled the most barrels in a week. It was a very hollow honour, and not worth killing yourself for. I have seen women count other crews' barrels for fear they had been beaten!

Von Richter and Van Zelius and the other big German exporters strutted about everywhere. They either lived aboard the *Earl*, when it stayed a couple of days, or aboard their own steam yachts. After June, the Klondykers arrived to ship the herring over to Germany. There were also Russian merchants with mouthfuls of gold teeth. They made fortunes exporting herring to Russia.

Though Sanders Watt, the coopers' apprentice, rapped us up for work at 5 a.m. and we often worked into the early hours of the next morning, we still found time to enjoy ourselves. Running up and down the piers on the railway bogies was always great fun. On Sundays, we walked up to Haroldswick, the northernmost post office in the British Isles, to send home a few cards. I remember a crowd of us calling at the Kirk beyond the head of the loch one Monday afternoon. The door was open and a group of Highland women sat on a pew to rest their feet. Among the group was Christy, a wifie who was known to have swopped her waterlogged tubs for other women's dry ones when their backs were turned! The wet ones were of course much harder to lift. "Bengies Bella", one of Sottie Noble's quines and a born comedian, went into the pulpit and preached a sermon on the stealing of the tubs after she spotted Christy with her friends. Bella said in a sanctimonious voice, "All the sinners who have been stealing the tubs will be cast into the bottomless pit! Satan is in our midst, he has Christy McLeod in his grip! First she will be hanged and then she will be drowned and then she will get a far worse death!"

There were two big houses nearby. Sandison had a huge house above the pier called 'Springfield'. I don't know why but we all called it "The Lady's". On the way to the shop we passed the doctor's house, another mansion, Muness House. A whale's jaw bones formed an archway outside. A Mrs Irvine had an old croft hard on the shore and near the huts stood the old thatched housie where Robbie Tamson lived. If that place could speak! My father said it was there before the herring boom, when Balta was a centre for the great line fishing.

A good gutter could gut and grade 60 to 70 herring a minute. We couldn't reach that speed yet but we were getting closer to it. As the salt melted, the herring fell in the barrel and it had to be filled up again and branded. The first pickle was poured out and replaced by fresh. It was hard work rolling full barrels and stacking them three tiers high.

Frank Ewen would say, "It is time you quines were in your beds, it will not be that gallivanting at 5 o'clock in the morning!" Did we go to bed? Not on your life! We climbed up on the rafters to spy on the Wick women. They were a good bit older than us and used to sit on their kists kissing and cuddling their boyfriends. They were on one side and the Cairnbulg and Inverallochy girls were on the other. We saw some rare sights at Balta!

It was an age of music and song and nearly every hut had a melodian. With the long light, the birds singing, the rolling sea and the smell of the tar and brine, we thought we had the world in our arms. But it all passed so quickly. At the end of July we were packed and ready to face the Roost again, this time on our way south for the Broch fishing.

I was back home and under parental supervision. My wings were clipped!

John Ewen had two curing yards in the Broch. I worked at the one in School Street, where the council houses now stand. Its spoot-holes were in Mid Street. The other yard was on the Quarry Road with its spoot-holes along the Castle Braes. Ewen shared that yard with McKenzie, a Stornoway curer.

Miss Gladwell came regularly to see my parents, and I remember when Bob's wife, Agnes, died Miss Gladwell said her funeral service. It was one of the most beautiful services I ever heard. Agnes had worked hard all her days and was

well liked. I remember the enormous crowd singing the
"Rugged Cross". Her son, young Robert, was the same age
as me.

Our neighbours Kit and Willie were quiet folk. They
emigrated to America just before the First World War and
recently their granddaughter came to see me. The couple
who replaced them fought like two cats. I once saw her
crown him with a bronze horse! Everybody was glad to see
that pair away to Aberdeen. Sandy Crawford and his wife
Maggie Stewart were the next to live in the house. They were
good neighbours. An old mannie lived in the housie at the
front along with a country couple with six sons and a
daughter the same age as me. They were known as the "Curly
Locks" from New Pitsligo, one of the many families to come
in from the country at that time. The mother became an
expert at fisher work.

Mary McLeod lived across the street. She had four
sisters and a brother - my second cousins. "Gamrie Donald",
Mary's father, I remember well. He was a genuine Christian
man and I see him now sitting on their big kist playing his
harp and singing:

"Glory to his name, for he is aye the same,
Though earthly freens and freenships melt awa.
I can aye depend on him, tae gang through thick and thin,
For I hae proved that Jesus is the best freen o' a'."

Old Nancy was at the other side, another good
neighbour. As bairns we gathered at the gable of her house.
All the folk west of Nancy's house were good friends, and we
all did what we could for each other. Peter Wilson, always
known as "Peter Bainie", was a Portessie man who married
a Broadsea woman. We went in and out of each others'
houses all the time. Our doors stood open all day. The Lovies
were also great friends. They were related to me on my

granny's side and lived in number 84, where I live now. Several members of that family were lost when the Aberdeen trawler *Stream Fisher* struck the rocks at Cove.

"Old Bett", a St. Combs wifie, and her daughter Maggie were hard working women who had both been widowed early. Jeannie Geddes, my mother's cousin, came to stay with them when her two daughters went into aristocratic service. One of the girls had a son fathered by a Saltoun offshoot who was later killed in South Africa. Young Willie was brought up in London by a family named Watson. He went through public school to become a Second Lieutenant and, like so many others of his rank, was killed in the First World War while still in his 'teens. I have a drawing Willie did of the Fraserburgh lighthouse when he was a lad.

Willie Geddes

The Broch was a wonderful place in the late summer of 1910. A beehive of industry. At dinner time oilskin kwites lay at every door in Broadsea. Whole families of quines were at the herring; we were the gutting machines then.

The Broch Harbour was a magnificent sight when the German and Russian Klondykers joined the huge herring fleet. The Scandinavian stave boats with cargoes of barrel timber were aye on the go. When the season was at its height, the coopers often had to start work at two o'clock in the morning to make up their quota. There were huge piles of new barrels everywhere. My it was hard work! The men laboured for hours on end at their fires, the sweat just pouring down their faces. Two of my brothers were coopers and every night they came home with their clothes soaked with sweat. We often saw the young coopers' apprentices carrying stacks of heavy barrel lids on their heads. It was a part of their daily routine. James McLean, a Broadsea apprentice, died from meningitis when he was sixteen. Many said the illness had been caused by his work.

Chapter 5
'A ROARING TRADE'

As Fraserburgh prospered, another near neighbour, Rosehearty, declined. Many Rosehearty fishers came into the Broch for the fishing, along with the great gangs of gutting girls from an endless list of Scottish coastal towns and villages, and a good sprinkling of Irish and English folk. Peterhead had the same stir.

Downtown, the Broch's high kilns spewed out kipper reek. It wasn't an unpleasant smell, but it penetrated every neuk and cranny. Most kilns had those huge cowls that turned with the direction of the wind. Spring and Wilson had kilns at Broadsea and, in Albert Street, Cadora's kilns and gutting yard employed mostly English girls from Yarmouth and Lowestoft. Cardno had a closed in yard in Albert Street with 100 crews, and Irvine had the same on the Charlotte Street side. There were another two curers at the bottom of Albert Street and, in Commerce Street, the Bruces had 100 crews.

There was a kind of snobbery among the coopers' wives who thought it superior to live in the houses Bruce built for his men in Charlotte Street. Most of the big curers kept flats for their married men. Dickson built flats for his coopers at Caroline Place. Lowe had 80 crews in School Street. Paul Hendry employed 40 crews and next door to him John Ewen had 80. Abercrombie Davidson in Hanover Street had 30 crews and Bain in Cross Street had the same. From Broadsea to Kinnaird Head there was a solid line of herring yards, and a whole host of others stretched from the harbour to the Broch beach.

The girls' huts occupied every spare inch of ground, even in the curers' gardens. There were huts all the way from Broadsea to the lighthouse. They even had them on the

A. Bruce & Co., Commerce Street.
Bain & Co., Barrasgate.
J. & A. Blackhall, Do.
Bisset & Co., Denmark Street.
A. & J. Bisset, Broadsea.
Wm. Bruce, Do.
Jas. Buchan, Do.
T. P. Burnett, North Street.
    Do.   Reclaimed Ground.
Wm. Burnett, Do.
A. Buchan & Co., Do.
J. & T. Burnett, Do.

J. Cardno & Son, Albert Street.
Jas. Cheyne, Do.
J. & J. Crawford, Do.

Davidson & Sons, Reclaimed Ground.
A. B. Davidson, Hanover Street.
Duncan, Do.
Wm. Duthie, Castle Street.
John Duthie, Duke Lane.
John Dickson, Castle Street.
Wm. Downie, Barrasgate.
A. L. Duncan, Denmark Street.
I. & J. Dunbar, Do.

John. Ewen & Sons, School Street

Wm. Fraser, Duke Brae.
Forbes & Co.,

E. Gordon, Quarry Road.
R. Gordon, Do.
Gunther & Co., Park Street,

Paul Hendry, Mid Street.

Johnston & Co., Park Street.
    Do.   Reclaimed Ground.

Wm. Low, School Street.
James Low, Duke Lane.

P. McConnachie, College Bounds.
Maconochie Bros. Ltd., Kinnaird Head.
C. McDonald, Reclaimed Ground.
C. Mitchell, Do.
J. Mitchell &. Sons, Do.
Wm. Miller & Co., Barrasgate.
John McKenzie, Quarry Road.
Wm. May,
Wm. McCombie, Broadsea.
W. R, Massie & Sons, College Bounds
C. & W. Massie, Broadsea.
A. Milne & Son, Balaclava.
G. Milne & Co., Reclaimed Ground.
Mitchell & Sim, Castle Street.

Wm. Noble &. Co., Albert Street.
Wm. Noble, Do.
A. R. Noble, North Street.

P. R. Paterson, Son, & Co., Barrasgate

A. M. Ritchie, Balaclava.

G. C. Stephen, Do.
Stephen & Co., Park Street.
H. Simpson, Do.
Jas. Stevenson, Reclaimed Ground.
Scottish Russian Herring Co. Do
Alex. S. Sinclair, Denmark Street.
Alex. Skinner, Do.
Jos. Stephen, Balaclava.

J. M. Thomson, Barrasgate.
Thomson & Son, Do.
Lewis Thomson, Denmark Street.
W. R. Trail, Quarry Road.

James Wood, Do.
Watt & Co., Park Street.
A. Watt & Co., Balaclava.
T. Whyte & Son, North Street.

Kipperers and Freshers.
T. Brown & Sons, North Street.
G. Bradbury, Balaclava.
Burnett Bros., Albert Street,

Martin Connolly, College Bounds.

J. M. Davidson, Denmark Street.

Wm. Gillings, Fish Market.

Inkson & Tozer, Quarry Road.
Harry Inkson, North Street.

Kelsall Bros., Denmark Street.

George Smith, Do.
Alf. Spring & Co., Albert Street.
George Tarbor, Railway Station Yard
Stephen & Co.

Herring Exporters.
Jas. A. Thomson & Co.
Jas. S. Davidson.
Gunther & Co.
Wm. Leslie & Co., Limited.
Andrew Smith, and Schultze.
H. Dinesmann, Son & Co.
James Pittendrigh.
H. Wantzelius & Co.
S. B. Berkhahn.
Cardno Taylor, & Co.
William Simpson,
Paterson, Son & Co.

Curers in Fraserburgh
Fraserburgh Herald, June 28th 1910.

Castle Green. They stretched along the front from the railway station right to the Esplanade (the Esplanade was not the elaborate place it is today). Then there were what we called the "penny curers", who worked in a small way with only a handful of crews. It was so easy to make money through sweated labour in those days. In 1910, there were more curers about the place than I can remember, with yards tucked away in Frithside Street, High Street, Cross Street and even on Broadsea Shore. The shop keepers in the Broch and Peterhead must have done a roaring trade in the herring season! I often wish I could turn the clock back to those happy days.

Hundreds of horsemen came in from the country to cart the herring from the boats to the yards. They brought their own horses and carts and lived in bothies. The atmosphere in the town was very special and the young horsemen always looked forward to the herring fishing when they could leave their farm chores behind for a few weeks. It was hard work but never dull. John Ewen took on three horsemen for the summer; two brothers, Danny and Jim Johnstone from a farm just outside the Broch on the Strichen road, and a shy laddie, Willie Milne, from up the Tyrie way. He was an intelligent young man who one day planned to go to Canada. All three were expert horsemen and very likeable young men. I think they were students. We came to know most of the farm loons: they worked hard and joined in all the fun. There was a marked difference between the farmers' sons who came to drive the herring and farmers' daughters who wouldn't have looked at us. They thought themselves superior in some way.

Our three horsemen lived in a bothy above the stables on Mid Street (there's a carpet shop there now). I remember it was decorated with bright coloured rosettes from the horse shows. John Ewen asked us to clean the bothy from time to time and we were happy to do so. They were very decent

lads, no swearing or bawdy news. Older wifies would say
things to make them blush! When Mary's mother, Onty's
Maggie Ann, or my mother came down to us with a cup of
tea, they would give the horsemen a cup and a piece of loaf
and jam. Other carters would curse and bann and wish they
were in their beds instead of carting herring at midnight. The
bothy always smelt of sweaty socks and, as the loons didn't
get home to their farms at weekends, some of the girls would
take home their shift and wash it. At the end of the fishing,
they thanked us and said what a wonderful experience it all
had been, a lot better than working with their fathers' all
summer for nothing at all.

   The horsemen fared well in the herring yards - some
even found wives and settled happily in the Broch - but sadly
this was not the case for our lads. Willie Milne never saw
Canada: he was killed with the Gordon Highlanders in
France when he was 19. Danny and Jim suffered the same
fate. I think one was 20 and the other 22 - the Flowers o' the
Forest. What a scandalous waste. Those laddies worked for

John Ewen for three summers. They chose coopers who were quiet and kind to the women, not the short tempered brutes who cursed and swore at the least little thing. I was fortunate in that respect. Most of my employers were decent people, both at the herring and in service. Though I always had scab wages, I never got the bad usage some girls got. At service in the Broch the bad employers were well known and shunned. They were constantly changing staff.

The forest of masts and funnels in the Broch Harbour was a sight to see! Waiting for the boats to come in, we would be knitting. To have idle hands, even for a moment, was unforgivable.

Herring girls' bothies stretched from Broadsea all the way along the Castle Braes. Some were built of stone, like the shells of dwelling houses, with no lining. Others were temporary wooden huts like the ones we all used at Balta. When the season was at its height I've seen huts on the edge of the breakwater! As we lay in our beds at home on a Friday night we could hear the melodian music from the huts across the bay as the fishers danced into the early hours of Saturday morning. We had to be in by ten on Saturday night and, if we were not needed at the yards, everything stopped at midnight.

Paddy McColl, a boy from the west of Ireland, sheeled herring in the farlane. He sang all the Irish songs for us, and what a voice he had. Everybody was entranced when he sang 'Calling Me Home'. We sang all the Sankey hymns as we slaved away. It cheered us no end, but maybe not as much as when our mothers came along with a jug of hot tea and a sandwich! Mrs Brown, a wifie from the High Street, went around the yards with her three daughters selling tea and tasty home made meat pies. Mrs Brown's determination paid off and the proceeds of her tea and pie sales sent all three of her daughters to university. Alice, Mabel and Walta graduated as teachers. Alice taught me in the North School, and later taught my son and daughter. Mrs Brown's son, James, became a doctor in London.

My mother always filled her girnal with meal bought direct from the Watermill. In days past all the grain grown on the Philorth estate was milled there - we called it the "Mullie". The wheel was driven by a sluice and a rapid burn from the dam. The miller's house was on a little island with burns on both sides. I remember the meal had a delicious burnt taste; it's not like that now. My mother and I, each with a pillowcase, went to fill our oak barrel. I still have it yet. I remember a little loonie dabbling his feet in the burn. His shoes and socks were just soaked. He was so young he couldn't say his name. Mother was afraid the loonie would be drowned. We spoke to the woman from the mill house but she didn't know who he was. She said he had been there all day but didn't come from the Chapelhill or the Watermill cottar houses. We took the loonie home and gave him his supper, and then left him with my sister while we went to the police. Eventually his mother, a Gamrie woman, came to collect him. The boy had wandered a mile and a half out of the Broch. My was she pleased to see him!

The School Street yard had open farlanes, like square boxes low on the ground. They were murder to work at. We were bending all the time and constantly raking with our scoops to bring the herring nearer. The carrying tubs were heavy with rough rope lugs and tipping them into the roosin' tubs was really hard on our hands. Katrine Ann was a good packer and, even though we were still regarded as a "learner crew", we were getting up some speed. Mary McLeod was a fast gutter, so we had a good season and it was with much pleasure that I handed my mother three gold sovereigns.

Britain was still on the gold standard and everybody was paid in sovereigns. In the Edwardian era Britain was the richest nation in the world but, although we had a vast colonial empire and controlled the bulk of world trade, I'm afraid the work force was treated no better than the natives abroad. In school we learned of the "Empire Builders" - missionaries, explorers, and businessmen of great stature - but to my generation, who fought two World Wars, our rewards have been less than creditable. The slums in the Broch were a disgrace! In 1910, world banking was controlled from London, but precious little came our way. It was the fierce independence and natural dignity of folk that carried us through.

Three St. Combs girls lived in "Kallie's Alex's" garret. We used to set out for work together in the morning. The summers seemed much warmer then. It was a long day and often we were scarcely in our beds at night when an impudent halfling loon would come rapping at the door telling us to dress and get down to the yard for a late boat. It might be ten o'clock in the evening, but still we went running. We tied our fingers with strips of a flour bag to protect them while we worked. The coarse salt could turn a tiny cut into a gaping festered wound in no time at all.

As the Broch fishing drew to a close and the last barrel was filled up and sealed to the Fishery Officer's satisfaction, it was time to pack our kists once more and head for Lowestoft.

The long Fraserburgh train was coupled to the Peterhead special at Maud junction. Out of Aberdeen the carriages swayed as we criss-crossed the points and Craiginches Prison zoomed past. There were vans for the curers' own horses. Everybody in Broadsea knew "Prince", Jimmy Cheyne's horse, and Prince knew everybody. He would put his head in the door to get a piece on his way to the grass in the Waul Park. Jimmy Alex Crawford also had a friendly horse, "Dobbin", which he always took to the East Anglia fishing.

Our kists had been packed with our wellington boots and oilskins laid on the lid, covered with packsheets and securely roped. Roping a kist was a skilled job and, though the coopers helped us when they could, we often had to manage ourselves. It was heavy work, constantly turning a full trunk up on end.

Winter came early, with snow and ice on the roads around Lowestoft. We were in John Ewen's Havelock yard, down at the beach. The icy wind from the sea went right into our bones and we often had to break the ice on our barrels in the early morning darkness. The sore festered hands were terrible. Filling up in the early morning I have seen many girls faint with the cold. The Wick women advised us to take a drop of the hard stuff in our tea but we didn't have any.

We had to climb the steps at the Scores when we went to our digs for dinner near the 'Highlight'. Mrs Allerton was our landlady - a nice woman. Her nephew, Bill Cooper, was a smoker with Kelsall. He later married and settled in the Broch. I liked Lowestoft and explored it fully. We all enjoyed our trip over to Norwich too, a fine town with a market and a good shopping centre. Nevertheless, we were glad when the fishing ended and we were homeward bound with our boxes of rock and gifts for everyone.

There were no corridors on those long trains. Our only sanitation was a treacle tin and, with thousands of women on board, many a poor railway worker must have been drenched! By the start of the Great War corridor trains were put on for us. I remember once we stopped at North York station. The sign there just said 'N. York'. Everybody was half asleep when a Bredsie wifie, startled by the jolt, opened her eyes and shouted, "Michty! We hae landed in America!"

The new corridor trains brought fun and joy to our long journeys. We sang with gusto and stamped our feet to melodian music as the train rumbled through the night:

"Come along, come along, let us foot it out together
Come along, come along, be it fair or stormy weather.
Wi' the hills o' hame before us, and the purple o' the heather,
Let us sing in happy chorus come along!"

Lowestoft Harbour, c.1910

In the still night air the music carried well. I remember passing through Waverley Sation and hearing a platform porter telling someone that the fishers were all drunk! This, of course, wasn't true. We never took drink, we just sang till we fell asleep.

When we arrived in Aberdeen, we had a look round the shops and made a holiday of it. We always went to see Granny Kirsty at Cornhill Hospital and, if she felt like it, we'd take her into the town for tea. Granny saw us onto the bus at Watson Street and we would watch her walk back to the hospital gates. She never looked back after we'd said goodbye. Granny Kirsten seemed to keep abreast of all that went on, but I often wondered what she was thinking, poor soul, a prisoner of circumstance.

The night we came home every mother would have a special treat waiting, like mutton chops or stewed steak, or something we weren't accustomed to.

Our parents couldn't afford to keep us at home, so we found what work we could for the winter months. I was skiffy to Mrs Anderson, the Baillie's wife, in a house called 'Dalvreck' in Grattan Place. Bengie's Kirsten was skiffy to Mrs Reid, an architect's wife, in Victoria Street. We both started work at six o'clock, so we set out together at about half past five. It was eerie at that time of the morning.

My cousin Betsy Taylor was skiffy at the MacDougall's house, 'Blytheswood', at the corner of Strichen Road. Mary McLeod was skiffy to the Calders in Seamount, on the edge of the Links. Unknown to me then, that house had once belonged to my future husband's parents. We left Kirsten at the Hexagon and Betsy had a key to let herself in a side door on King Edward Street. Mary carried on to Seamount, beside Queen Victoria's Jubilee Fountain, where the War Memorial now stands, and I went on a short distance into Grattan Place. There were gaps between some of the houses in those days where the curers' ponies grazed.

The street lighting wasn't as good as it is now. In high winds the gas lights blew out and that could be really dangerous. I was trusted with my own key and let myself in through the back door. The furniture in the house was beautiful. Mr Anderson had a prosperous cabinet maker's business and employed a half dozen tradesmen who produced beautiful stuff that lasted a lifetime. The men were skilled artists but were paid with sweeties. All our furniture was made locally in those days.

My first job was to rake out and blacklead the kitchen range and the drawing room fire. Then I made breakfast for the family; two rashers of bacon and a fried egg with sausage and tomato. I had prepared the porridge the night before. I then woke them up and waited at the breakfast table. They had a son and a daughter, a year or two younger than me, at the Broch Academy. I think they both went in for medicine and moved out to South Africa. The girl never spoke to me, and the lad only spoke to me once. He asked if I would blanco his tennis shoes when he forgot to put them out with all the others. After they had gone to school, Mrs Anderson gave me my breakfast in the kitchen; tea and toast with a bowl of porridge and a little bowl of milk. She was a daughter of Nibloe the baker from Kirk Brae, a firm woman but never nasty like some of the wifies in that gate end. She called me Chrissie. She was an excellent baker and a credit to her father's trade.

Chapter 6
'THE BREDSIE WARRIORS'

It was a long weary day and my list of jobs was endless. I could see why so many girls in regular domestic service would have married anybody to get away from it! How we all longed for the fishing to start again. I was paid half a crown on Saturday for my week's work. I always ate in the kitchen. The bedrooms had bay windows with lovely views across the bay to Cairnbulg point.

Sometimes we would be a little after eight in finishing some jobbie, so the four of us did not walk home together every night. Mrs Anderson told me that I must never answer the front door unless I was in formal maid's clothing, and never in an apron with my sleeves rolled up. My mother, quite rightly, wouldn't let me buy all the different dresses servants had to wear. The pay we got did not cover the price of those things.

One day the bell rang and Mrs Anderson answered the door. I was polishing the varnished stair treads either side of the Red Turkey stair carpet. I had to remove the brass stair rods and polish them too. The door brasses were done before anybody was up - the neighbours must *never* see a servant at the front door. Mrs Anderson was talking to a woman at the door. It was none other than my neighbour, "Bathie Curly Locks"! She was forward and bold. "We are very poor," she said, "have you anything to give us please?" Mrs Anderson produced a loaf. I don't know how old it was, but I heard the thud as she dropped it into Bathie's basket!

Cranna, the harbour treasurer, lived in Victoria Street. His wife always addressed her servants by their surnames. One day she said to a Bredsie girl, "Noble, if anybody calls, show them into the drawing room." Mrs Cranna was rather upset when Noble showed Meg Pom, a vagrant wifie, into the drawing room!

There were no hoovers then - it was all elbow grease. We put tea leaves on the carpets to bring up the dust. There was no wall to wall carpeting. Mr Anderson always had a lot of mail to open at the breakfast table. He spoke to his family about South African gold, Rhodesian copper, and stocks and shares, of which I knew nothing at all. Mr Anderson was a senior Ballie. I thought just how selfish Fraserburgh Town Council had always been - they abused the Broadsea people. It was something very old and very bitter, the same as any nation or people held in subjection to another. We spoke a different dialect from the town and our whole outlook was completely alien to theirs. In 1420, Fraser of Philorth had given the Broadsea fishings to his daughter as a part of her wedding dowry and, after the creation of the Burgh of Fraserburgh, nearly two centuries later, the Frasers bought them back. It was a thriving fishing place until about 200 years ago when 36 fishermen were lost; two thirds of the male population! The women left had to provide for the bairns till they grew up. The town's folk looked on them enviously for some reason. To start with they had stolen the common lands which stretched from College Bounds to the Gallowhill.

All the sewers ran out at Broadsea and the herring goor and offal was tipped over the braes with no regard for the villagers. All the gutting yards were erected there after the big herring boom, so too were the gut factory and killing house. The middens for human dung lay along the Broadsea foreshore. Fishers were regarded as the lowest of the low.

Gang warfare was rife in my childhood, but the girls, of course, did not get involved. We were the "Bredsie Warriors". "The Shore Tykes" were our allies and "The Hungry Brochers" our sworn enemy. Many a pitched battle took place in the vicinity of the Alexandra Hotel! Under no circumstances would we ever claim to be Brochers. To call us that was an insult. We could see how the Town Council had connived to keep the south side "nice".

"The Bredsie Warriors"

The following May we were at Holmsgarth, half way between Lerwick and Gremista. The Roost was as bad as ever! Curing stations stretched for four miles, each with their own jetty for landing herring. Bressay Island, on the other side of the sound, was also a mass of curing stations.

John Noble, our head cooper, lived at Lancaster House in Victoria Street. He was a member of the recently inaugurated meeting of the Open Brethren, so swearing was strictly forbidden. Our station was quite flat, but further from the shore they stood on steep slopes and there were hundreds of huts on the high ground that skirted the North Road. We knew all the shops in Lerwick - often they would give us a cup of tea when we gave them our custom.

It was a really busy port with dozens of ships flying foreign colours. The Mitchells from the Broch had a barrel factory and gutting station. They had a wooden bungalow and their two daughters, Marjory and Agnes, came up for holidays. They brought motor bikes with them, very rare then. The sound was a mass of pleasure craft and the Queen's Hotel was full of German and Russian exporters, all flashing their gold teeth! The Russians wore fur hats, even at the height of a scorching summer.

German bands came ashore. They were good musicians, but many said their real purpose was to map the bays and voes around the islands. The young ones wore short leather breeks and always had a notebook and pencil.

Gamrie Lerwick was a poor place. Most of its occupants were North East folk who had settled there during the days of the great line fishing. Their homes were simple wooden huts that had changed little over the years. My father and my sister were at Balta that year, and I was pleased to be in Lerwick, and out of their gaze.

The hut next door was occupied by three nice girls from Johnshaven and Gourdon; they called it "Gurdon". It was a lot less crowded at Lerwick, only three to a hut, yet for some reason we didn't have the same sense of freedom we had at Baltasound.

In 1911, forty five thousand people were engaged in the Scottish herring fishing. The same was going on at Castle Bay in Barra, Stornoway, the Isle of Man, Stronsay and Wick. My sister Margaret was 10 years my senior and had worked in all those places, and a good many more in northern and southern Ireland. We started at 6 a.m. and were seldom finished before midnight. Irish loons emptied the herring kits for us that year - they were fine company.

Dower from Wick had the station next to ours. He was a funny mannie, always laughing and joking with the quines.

Jock Troup, the preacher, a nice laddie Gunn and a boy Swanson were apprentices with Dower. We were a very close knit community and got to know each other well. We knew all the Buckie quinies who worked for Shearer. It was pleasant out at Greenhead, but a long walk from the town.

One Monday afternoon we had no filling up, so the whole crowd of us, coopers and all, hired a charabanc in Lerwick and drove over to Scalloway. It was a lovely June day and we took plenty of dry sticks to make a fire on the shores of East Voe. John Noble said grace before our grand picnic on the grassy banks. We explored the old castle with Jock Stewart, a cooper, and his wife Lizzie Bo, the coopers' cook. The trip only cost us a shilling each.

With the summer sun, fresh sea air and hard labour, the fishing passed like a drink of water. When we boarded the *St. Sunniva* for the voyage home, nobody could have imagined that the small steamer would soon be taking part in a conflict which would cost the lives of 230,000 merchant seamen. Stromness was an interesting old place with gable ended houses that seemed to go on forever. Like Lerwick and Kirkwall it had been a port of call for our ancestors at the whaling. We went ashore and bought some china crested keepsakes before the last leg of our journey across the Moray Firth.

It was good to be back home again. We sat down to a nice supper at a table laid with a white cloth and gave everyone our news. The Broch fishing was getting under way and I was to start work at Quarry Road. We could see the yard from our house.

The Broch was so busy the curers had to sign up extra crews from New Pitsligo, and cottar and crofter quines from the country. One of those girls later became Mrs Park and remained my good friend for life.

Boats under sail, July 1911.
The Fraserburgh registered 'Sapphire' of Cairnbulg, centre.

For many years the Skinners, a family from Cromarty, lived in my Granny Poll's but end. Their granddaughter, Jeannie Watson, was a student at the University of British Columbia - a fine scholar judging by the letters she wrote. Jeannie loved the fishing here and came over three years running to take arles for the summer season. She married a schoolmaster in Vancouver and they had a son who was in the navy during the Second World War. In 1942, he came to Broadsea to try to fork us out but wasn't sure who he was looking for. I was sorry I didn't see him but was pleased to hear that May Crawford at number 32 had given him his tea. His mother's cousin, Kate Noble, was living just along the road, but he didn't know about her.

John Ewen's huts were in Quarry Road and our horsemen, the Johnstone brothers and Willie Milne, lived on the ground floor of a half house at the end of the row. They shared their rooms with the Irish labourers. Mary Buchan's cookhouse was in a back room through the middle door of the same building. She was a widow from Inverallochy and looked after the boys well.

John Ewen's horses.

The Ewens were good folk to work for. We never had the short change problems some of our friends had to put up with. When Frank Ewen asked us if we would like to go to Campbeltown for a few weeks we all jumped at the chance. The west coast town, in a beautiful Highland setting, sheltered by Davaar Island, was as busy as the Broch, with island passenger steamers coming and going all the time. We gutted on the quayside and had digs in a housie at Lochend. Our landlady was a kind wifie: she always had plenty of hot water ready for us when we got home, however late that was.

They were those nice big Loch Fyne herring. Once sprinkled with salt they were as firm as boards and it didn't take a lot to fill the barrel. We had our photo taken sitting on an old stone cross in the middle of the main street. There were big houses all over the place. We pitied the servant quinies in their formal dress at the doors. There must have been coalmines nearby - coalboats were constantly loading up at the quay and, if the wind was in a certain direction, the smell of a distillery pervaded the whole town.

We were always ready to pack our bags at short notice and go to where the herring were coming ashore. I enjoyed my short time in Campbeltown, and my first look at Glasgow, but soon we were on our way home again to prepare for Yarmouth.

A long horse drawn lorry came to Broadsea to take our kists to the station. There were kists at every door. Nearly every house owned a fishing boat and nearly every house sent girls to the fishing. Our mothers were at the station to see us off - the long special train stretched as far as the signal box at the Bathalonian Brae. Wifies were lined along the railway fence as far as the high brig by the kirkyard, all waving and shouting as the train pulled away. At Maud Junction we waited half an hour for the Peterhead special to join us, just enough time for a quick cup of tea in the Station Hotel.

Maud was the nerve centre of Buchan. A huge cattle market developed at the railway junction where livestock and crops from all over the district were gathered for shipping to the continent from Peterhead or Fraserburgh. Daily chains of box wagons loaded with fish for the English markets passed through Maud, and so did the thousands of fishers on their annual journey south. It was a sad day for Buchan when Beeching axed the North East lines, especially now with all the oil boom traffic on the roads.

The farming folk were well served by the line. Friday's Aberdeen train was aye full of farmers bound for the cattle mart at Kittybrewster - jolly men, with a dry sense of humour. As the crowded train belted over the Forth Brig we all made a wish and threw a bawbee into the Firth. My wish was always the same - may I never die of cold! The Tay Brig was a different matter. Though it had been several years since the dreadful disaster, the memory was always with us when we crossed it.

It was night when we passed through the English towns. There were no dining cars on our trains. They would have been too expensive for us anyway, so everybody took plenty of food with them. We all kept hens at home and a couple were usually set aside and fattened for a special treat on the Yarmouth train. Cold chicken and tomato. Our mothers looked after us well.

Arriving at Vauxhall Station, I noticed the Yarmouth tongue was more easily understood than the Lowestoft one. There were a lot of dark haired folk with flashing teeth. We had digs in the Row at the back of the town hall, a long walk from the yard at the South Denes. The people who lived in those narrow lanes of slum houses were very poor. I remember one of the Rows, 'Kitty Witches Row', was little more than two feet wide.

The kippering yards were built hard against the ancient flint town walls. We used to walk through Blackfriar's Tower on our way to the Denes. Bloaters were very popular down south but never really took off in Scotland. They were herring or mackeral dipped in brine and lightly smoked. With the entrails left inside them they had to be eaten right away.

My sister had good digs in Howard Street. I remember when a St. Combs man kicked up a din one Saturday night, the wifie threw out all her boarders! Robbie Chalmers, a carter, took their kists on his lorry and, with the girls on top, he drove it through the Salvation Army ring on the Middelgate on Sunday morning! The police gave the Scots boys some terrible hidings for the least thing.

Fishing boats covered the river all the way past the Town Hall to the Haven foot bridge over to Gorelston. We crossed the river by walking over the boats that lay side by

Yarmouth Denes

side. The English boats went out on Sunday night but the "Jocks", as they called them, did not. There were a lot of bonnie houses along the South Quay that took in lodgers. We were in Number Two Row. Next door lived Bella Noble, Dodie Gundy's daughter, her cousin Mary Mitchell and Lizzie Trail. Barbara Malley, Leebie Ellen Noble and Lily Watt stayed at the same place. They were all nice girls with a great sense of fun. I think Katrine Ann married shortly after that, and Mary McLeod and I had Lizzie Duthie from the shore to make up our crew.

What fun we had. "Fytie's Kirsten", "Babbie Donelly" and her auntie Betty were in the same Row. Babbie's bonnie fur Boa had been eaten by mice in the digs so she went out every night and lifted a cat off the street to put in the bedroom! Babbie, poor soul, eventually died in Yarmouth. She is buried in the wilderness at the end of Nelson Road.

The Yarmouth Council wouldn't allow the curers to build huts. They realised that a good boarding house trade would be more to their advantage. It was a blessing to the

town's economy. There were a lot of good shops in Broad
Row and a good shopping centre in King Street. Thousands
of tea sets must have been bought by the Scottish girls in King
Street Market. The Shetland women were very fond of those
thin eggshell Japanese tea sets and gave them pride of place
in their cabinets at home.

The Denes were tracts of open land between the river
and the beach. The Nelson Monument stood alone at the
centre but in the season it was surrounded by thousands of
stacked barrels. There was no shelter and the fierce wind
from the sea tore at our oilskins and froze our sore hands.

There were many attractions for visitors to Yarmouth
and, even in those far off days, the town had a cultivated
tourist market. The Winter Gardens had a long row of
pavilion shelters the Scots called, "the canoodling boxes". It
was there that the courting lads and lasses met. As 15 year
olds we were very nosy, and we often saw folk there who had
no right to be!

When the tide was in, walking the Brittania Pier was
like being on a big ocean liner. We went on the revolving
tower. The day King George V came down from Sandringham
we all went up the town to see him. He wore a coat with a
fur collar, and he needed it! The soldiers in the barracks at
the South Denes whistled at us as we walked past, but we
gave them no cut. Sometimes the Salvation Army band
played on Gorelston Beach. The Marine Parade was like a
glorified 'Aikey Fair'.

The big congregational kirk was packed every Sunday
night. We had to go early if we wanted a seat. The double
gallery was always full to overflowing; all the Scots folk met
there. The singing was beautiful.

Today, when I draw my old age pension, I think of all
the long hours we put in for scab wages. What a difference
it would have made if working class folk in those days had
only a pound a week more. It would have rescued so many

from a life of constant struggle.

Narrow horse drawn "troll" carts, like kitchen tables with wheels, were specially built to run up and down the narrow Rows. Vegetable and fruit merchants, and even a butcher, came up and down the Rows on their trolls and we often got a ride on an empty one. The roads in the Rows were covered with broken flint and had central gutters.

We never felt like strangers when we were working away from home. How could we when we constantly heard Cairnbulg and Buckie accents? We got to know thousands of folk over the years. In spite of the cold, we sang to our hearts content as our fingers moved to the motion of the gutting. The Irish and Gaelic girls were always singing. There were thousands of wicker sweels about the place - a sort of basket used by the English for measure. If I remember rightly there were three sweels to a cran. I didn't know a year that somebody didn't return home, either lost off the Yarmouth Roads or drowned in the river. Every year we each paid a couple of shillings to the Scottish Fishers' Funeral Fund, set up to take bodies home for burial and, as the years went by, I knew of many who were thankful for it.

Mrs Ford in Number Three Row boarded a lot of coopers. A girl came to her house one day to make up the voters' roll - lodgers, of course, were excluded. She asked Mrs Ford who lived there permanently, and the wifie told her Tommy Ford, Billy Ford and Roy Ford. The municipal election took place and voting papers for those eligible arrived in the post. "Tommy", "Billy" and "Roy", it turned out, were the landlady's cats! At her insistence, the three coopers that were lodging with her that year, Bett's William Noble, George Andrew Sheves and Peter Ritchie, voted with the cats' ballot papers. Mrs Ford was delighted when her candidate got in.

The rock factory did a roaring trade as we made ready for home. Charlie Tait stayed till Christmas - his was the last boat to sail for home. The fishermen were always helpful; they took our bulky luggage home for us. In earlier days the boats would go up the Ythan at Newburgh after the Yarmouth fishing to get mussels for the small lines. Ythan mussels were regarded as the best for line bait.

My winter job that year was skiffy to Mrs Noble in King Edward Street and she wasn't a bad mistress. Her late husband was John Noble from Broadsea. Their two sons still lived at home, both good looking lads. James had been at college in London and was temporarily in the fish trade. The daughter was very bigsy, but even the best of the the "well to do" Brochers only had to go back one or two generations to find their ancestors in a but 'n' ben! The Nobles had about two dozen cousins in Broadsea but I never saw any of them pay a visit. Mrs Noble had a kind manner. She told me to take my time polishing and, if I did it properly, it would stand for several days. I had porridge and milk for breakfast and sometimes a buttery roll. I fried bacon and eggs every day for the family, but they seemed to think servants didn't like bacon and egg, or maybe they thought it slowed us down too much! I got on well with Mrs Noble and she wanted me to stay on with her. She paid me the usual half-crown a week, which I passed on to my mother.

Once the fishing started, it was almost impossible to get a skiffy in the Broch. The better off had to depend on poor quinies coming in from the country for work. Some of them were actually starved. One of the girls made us laugh in the gutting yard. She had spent the winter at service in a large house on Strichen Road, and was so hungry one day that she smeared the toddler's mouth with an egg yolk and ate the egg herself! Today we're not paying for the sins of our fathers but the sins of our fathers' employers. When I left Mrs Noble she gave me an extra shilling with my last half-crown. I gave it to my mother. Her son James was a handsome soldier. He was killed in France late in the War.

His cousin, Freddie Crawford from Broadsea, was killed at the Somme.

My pal Kirsten was skiffy to Mrs Owen at the toolwork's houses. Her husband was the manager there. It was a long dark road for a quinie to walk at 5.30 in the morning, so she waited for the milk loons or the morning roll loons and they all went down the road together. Most of the front row of the toolwork's houses had servant girls who would all walk to work together. Working folk had to rise early to make a shilling. It was certainly a long weary day.

I was happy when the fishing season came around again and I was back on board the *St. Rognvald* and on my way to Baltasound. We were advised to eat soda scones to counteract the sickness and strangely enough it seemed to work, though I did feel more than a little squeamish when the steamer plunged and lurched its way through the Roost. North of Kirkwall the engines throbbed and the hull shivered, but it was not until we passed the Fair Isle that the scones were really put to the test! The smell of vomit was terrible, but I didn't spew. We were glad to glide up Balta Loch and berth at the Sandison Pier. The day was beautiful, cool and crisp, and the sun rose gently in a bonnie blue sky. The sailors on the warship cheered as we passed them.

Chapter 7
'SIMMER DIM AND THE MERRY DANCERS'

We had a hut at the end of the block where it was a bit less noisy. My father always went on about being careful with fire in the huts. True enough, those places would have gone up in seconds, the wood was so dry. In the 1930s my niece and her companions lost all their belongings when a whole block of huts burned to the ground at Stronsay.

Bain's cook was a 16 year old quinie from New Pitsligo. The poor child spilt a heavy iron pot of hot soup over her feet and was badly burned so we all pulled together to help with her chores. I remember she cried when the women dressed her feet. The other girls did all the washing for her. Folk were different then.

With a window on the front and one on the gable we could see all that was going on. For sanitation long trenches were dug for the men, a good distance up the hill, and surrounded by sacking. Spades were kept handy to fill in the earth as required. There were plenty of funny stories about sheep poking their heads through the sacking! The women's toilets were out on the staging, with direct access to the sea. Water was always scarce and I remember Lewis Thompson, a curer, had a small burn dammed for his own use. We often stole a bucket of water from it. One day a big row broke out between Thompson and Mary Cote. He didn't know what he had let himself in for. Mary always had the last word!

Sweat, toil, melodian music and dancing - the young coopers were always up to some devilment. At the weekend, the white tablecloth and the bonnie cups came out and we aye had a crowd in for tea. It was great fun. We would think up really daft things to do, like telling the boys to shout their girlfriends' names up the lum! Johnnie Noble and Colin McRae were our apprentices and Sottie's daughter Kirsten was their cook. She was married to Mary McLeod's uncle. At Sottie's lower station Nellie Pirie put the ladle in their pot of soup and fished out a shoe, the glue had melted and the heel had boiled off. That was dinner for six ruined and, with spare time so precious, that was not funny! Mrs McLeod gave them a jug of broth to make up for their lost lunch.

We had Nairn girls for neighbours, and through the wall on the other side were two crews from Embo. Only a thin wooden partition divided our huts, so we missed nothing. Dunbar's was the first station on the south side, opposite the little Huney Island. "Chay's Annie", "Tammie's Jeannie" and Annie Wattie were with Dunbar. Annie got letters from her brother and the others wondered why she always hid them so quickly. When the chance came, one of the girls had a quick look at one. It said, "Don't take up with the girls in the hut, take up with your cousin Rebecca."

The other three who shared our hut were Mary Ann Cameron, Elisabeth Watt and Magdalane Noble, the daughter of Cocky Noble, the Broadsea boat builder. Georgie Crawford was one of our apprentice coopers - he lived opposite the Alexandra Hotel in the Broch. Georgie was one of the thousands of young men to die in the horror of the Dardanelles.

We sang all night as we worked in the long 'Simmer Dim':

"For we a' love bonnie Jessie, she's the floore o' Inverness,
Nae a rose in a' the gairden, her beauty can possess,
There will be bonfires on the hillside, ye will hear the pipers play,
Should auld acquaintance be forgot, on Jessie's wedding day".

The *Sea Gleaner* was lying at Johns Ewen's wharf. The skipper was big Sanny Pum from St. Combs. They were carrying nets ashore on a barrow and we gave them a hand to spread them on the grass behind the station. The fishing was nearly over and the nets looked as though they had been dipped in lime. A lot of white soapstone was quarried at Balta for making chrome and talcum powder. On a wet day the stuff was so slippery you could have fallen and broken your neck! I wondered if there were large deposits of this stuff in the sea which made the nets white? When they were lifted the grass was covered with white powder.

Sanny Pum sent Arthur, his cook loon, up to Sandison's shop for cold roast beef, beetroot and tomatoes. When Arthur came back he told him to, "Fill the pan with eggs, just like ye wad dee tatties, and gie the quinies a gweed supper!" Arthur also brought us a huge bag of scones and some fresh Shetland butter. We had a lovely picnic on the grass.

We came back on the *St Magnus* and our two months at home just flew by. My brother John married Jane Crawford, and our house was renovated. The ceilings were heightened and a new wooden floor was laid and covered with linoleum from end to end. We had a big shed built at the back, new fireplaces fitted at both ends of the house and, best of all, we had our very own tap with running water.

My father came home one night with some dreadful news. A navy gunboat had gone clean through his nets. They were ruined! When the *Venture* turned turtle some ten years earlier all the gear had been lost and Willie Crawford, Jock Mosley's son, had given my father a few old nets to start again. For that my father was most grateful, but what would become of us now? Naval vessels had the right of way at sea and the Admiralty paid no compensation.

Thankfully, two good friends came to my father's aid. Some said the curer Alex Gordon was a shark. He may have been all that, and more, but he had good bits too. Without asking, he came and offered my father the money for half a fleet of nets to be paid off at the ordinary rate of interest, and George Walker, the fish salesman, did the same. The loans were repaid punctually and Alex Gordon gave my mother a half barrel of herring. George Walker gave her a wooden box of tea, courtesy of his son Bremner, a tea planter in Ceylon. My auntie Babbie's Bella had a grocer's shop in Noble Street and she let us have the boat's provisions on tick for a while. We were grateful to the Almighty for so many good friends. We had to work hard to get back on our feet, starting by curing and drying ling and haddock for Miller Ritchie. My mother mended nets and knitted ganseys. Every moment was spent trying to make a shilling. She even went out to do washing for folk. My father did extra jobbies too. They wore themselves out to pay off the debt and two years later we were free again. How my parents wished they hadn't spent their savings on renovating the house!

The yard was closed for four days after John Ewen's son Arthur died. He was only 23. It was 1912 and Danny Johnstone and Willie Milne were our horsemen again. I think Danny's brother had taken up his career. Danny's pal Jim Corbett from Watermill had recently lost his father and Danny had advised him to have a spell in the Broch before taking on the responsibility of the farm. Jim was a genuine boy and one of the best. He was only sixteen, but could certainly handle the horse. In later years, he always recognised us on the street and talked of the happy times. Jim shocked his family by marrying his mother's kitchen maid. She made him a first class wife. Her sister delivered our milk after her husband went off to the Second World War.

The nights were long and warm. We sang hymns at the farlane and all the latest songs. 'The Shade of the Old Apple Tree' and 'The Good Ship Yacky Hicky Dula' wafted over Broadsea Bay a dozen times a day. Trudging along the braes on our way home to bed we were tired but never dispirited. There was a large deep pool below the foghorn where the water changed with every tide. We were past the longest day and the last few hours of our shift were done under naphta lamp light. The oily smoke blackened our faces so the coopers and horsemen sometimes went to the pool for a midnight dip in the nude. One night, two Buckie quines from Eddie Gordon's huts hatched a plot to hide the young lads' clothes and towels while they were bathing, but they were spotted and a crowd of boys shot out of the pool after them. They caught the girls on the Castle Park and, still in the nude, carried them skirlin' back to the pool for a ducking!

Nobody could ever have dreamt that a year or two later most of those lads, so young and full of life, would have their names carved on war memorials.

It was the summer of 1913 and my father, I'm pleased to say, had a good fishing. I remember we got off work early to go to Miss Gladwell's picnic at Philorth. It was a beautiful estate before the dreadful fire. We went to Philorth on a horse lorry driven by one of Dickson's summer horsemen, a quiet country laddie called Argo. The following Saturday we went to the Salvation Army picnic at Brucklay.

Mrs Kafootershank, our Yarmouth landlady the year before, had her house full of men who were there to dredge the river, but we found good digs with Mrs Sutton in the Rows. She was a jewel of a wifie, kind and motherly to us young quinies. The poor soul lost her life in the blitz of the Second World War. Her children, Joey and Lizzie, were nice bairns. I remember when I asked Joey if the kettle was boiling, he said, "I don't know if it be boiling, but it be dancin' all right!"

The Denes, as usual, was freezing. The icy wind blew hard over the flat land and that year snow followed our train all the way back home. We had tin kettles and small spirit lamps, so we made tea on the homeward journey. Betty Lass, a very nice wifie from Charleston St. Combs, was in our carriage. She was married to an uncle of Sir William Duthie, MP for Banffshire, and her husband was a second cousin of my mother. To pass the time Betty read our tea leaves. She told Bengie's Kirsten that she was to meet a tall dark chap, and that I was to meet a fair one. It was all in fun. We used to visit Betty in her cute little housie, the last one in Charleston.

Arriving in Broadsea, Elizabeth Jane Noble, Skipper's daughter, opened her kist to find that out of devilment a cooper had popped in a bonnie blue willow pattern chanty pot. It was part of the Yarmouth landlady's bedroom set! It cost a lot of money to have it properly packed in that cork stuff boxes of grapes used to come in, and posted back to Yarmouth.

We were back among the noise of the coopers' hammers - the life blood of the Broch. On New Year's Day there was snow on the ground when we followed the Flute Band to Rosehearty. Against my will, and on the instigation of my father, I became servant to my uncle Donald and his wife Mary Duthie, who had started sheeling and baiting the small lines. All the work was done in a garden shed, and I hated it!

They had a beautiful new granite house at the end of Mid Street which in those days was surrounded by fields. My uncle had wanted my father to take on half of the house. What he had spent on 72 Broadsea could have been a good down payment. Alex Gordon offered my father a bond to build the house with his brother, but my father said he wanted to be carried out of the place where he was born if the sea did not claim him first. Alex Gordon was good in that way. He lent Kirsten's father the money to build a house on George Street. In our case, my mother and my uncle's wife would not have got on, so we were better off with our own front door.

The lines had to be carried in a scull on the top of my creel all the way to my uncle's boat, *Rosevine*, in Fraserburgh harbour. It was a life of utter servility. I made up my mind in no way would I ever marry a fisherman, though codlin blood ran through my veins. At the corner of Mid Street, by the door of the Clydesdale Bank, the scull caught the wall and the line fell down onto the street in a great tangled mess. A man passing kindly helped me red it up a bit. Uncle Donald was furious and really abusive. "You useless article", he roared, "go home and don't come back!" I told him that suited me fine! My father insisted that I went back to work but I refused.

I got a job filleting with Miller Ritchie. The winter of 1913 was even colder than usual and packing cart loads of white fish in ice was murder. Old Susie Murison was the boss and she kept us all on the ball. Bengie's Kirsten worked with me and, in spite of the hard cold work, we had a lot of laughs. There had been three heavy falls of snow and the roads and railways were blocked. The fish train couldn't get through for a while but the cold weather kept the fish as fresh as the day it came ashore. When the thaw came it filled up all the burns - there was no shortage of water then!

We had seen a lot of "Merry Dancers" shooting and

leaping in the northern sky; the borealis over Buchan is a wonderful sight. A gale always follows. Part of a fisherman's education is studying the weather. My late uncle William was an expert. By sniffing the sea air and looking at the clouds he could forecast exactly what weather lay ahead. We watched the geese from the Loch of Strathbeg and, if they turned in formation and headed back to the loch, we knew that bad weather was on the way.

The young girl who worked with us in Miller Ritchie's fish-house was not a fisher. She wore a tartan plaid all the time so we called her "Tartan Annie". She had been disowned by her well off parents and, although everybody was good to her, I always felt sorry for the girl. The staff were mostly older women, experts at the job. I was glad when May came around again and we were once more on our way to Baltasound. I was now 17 and had been well warned of the consequences of entertaining the boys. My mother told me not to become "Chicky for Chowie" - too far in with any particular one.

We sailed on the *St. Rognvald*, the same six girls in the same hut. We worked hard and enjoyed the fresh air. Always, a crowd came to tea at the weekend. My father and Donald McLeod kicked up a din when they heard a melodian playing one Sunday. It was, I'm pleased to say, in another hut. An extraordinary amount of German yachts came that year. It was 1913 and passports were not yet required. The Germans were painting and sketching everything. I realise now that they were spying.

Lizzie Duthie was a quiet girl - her father was from Inverallochy and her mother, Liz Scott, came from Eyemouth. Lizzie's brother Robert came to our hut a lot. Crowds of us used to gather in their house on Shore Street in the Broch - I don't know how Mrs Duthie put up with us! A young deckie called Alex Cowie from Portessie was paying attention to Mary, and Mary Ann Cameron had another deckie,

Andrew Walker, for a dancing partner. I got paired off with Boy Strachan, a deckie on his father's boat, the *Grace Darling*. The skipper was a proud mannie; his boat had cretonne curtains on the sleeping bunks and linoleum on the cabin floor. Poor Lizzie Duthie died in America when she was in her twenties. We got on well as a team. We sometimes helped the fishermen spread their nets. Jock Dyer and his brother David were Gamrie men - they had the *Jasper*. Jock sent a deckie up to the shop for a box of chocolates to hand round among the girls. We often gave the boys a dab of butter to help get the tar off their hands.

"The smeel of tar I feel it far, its sweeter than the roses,
My bonnie lad wi' tarry breeks, I long when he proposes,
My lad he is a fisherman, that's why I sing this sang,
He is gaun tae marry me, and that will nae be lang!"

We spread nets for Bobby Stephen from George Street and for Joe Watt of the *Gowanlea*. In return, the skippers made sure we got a good supper.

Folk were nervous of steamers after the disaster of the "unsinkable" *Titanic*. It had been more than a year since the tragedy, but there was still no legislation about lifebelts and boats and we were packed aboard like sardines! The Germans couldn't get enough herring; we were even packing torn bellies. I see now that they were laying in a stock of food for the terrible War they were about to launch on the world. There was plenty to do at Balta that year and the time passed very quickly.

Mrs Sutton took us in again down in Yarmouth. She allowed us to bake and was a real gem. We couldn't have found better digs, but it was not like that for everybody. It was my cousin Violet's first trip south and she was so cold in her digs that she had to get some of the men to saw up battens for firewood. When Violet put a log on the fire, the landlord was furious! "Another bloody log", he said, "at ten o'clock at night!" He didn't know what to say when Violet told him it was her own wood.

Chris Whyte was a beautiful stately girl and a grand worker. She had been late in getting crewed and could only find two learner Gamrie quinies. We all took a good laugh when she said, "Who am I landed with? Lightning and Thunderbolt!"

Fisher Quines at Yarmouth Denes.

BROADSEA AUCTION MART
• *Auctioneers & Valuators* •
Seatown of Broadsea, Near Fraserburgh

AGRICULTURAL AUCTIONS • GENERAL • LIVESTOCK
MACHINERY • GRASS PARKS • POULTRY & GAME
LAND & FARMS • SHOOTING & FISHING

MONTHLY SALES OF FURNITURE REMOVED FOR CONVENIENCE
FIRST TUESDAY OF EVERY MONTH • VIEWING 10AM DAY OF SALE
ROUP 12 NOON • TERMS CASH

...

LIVE STOCK SALES EVERY FRIDAY • ROUP COMMENCING 10AM
CASH OR VERIFIED A/C

...

EXCELLENT POTATOES • TURNIPS • HAY & STRAW DELIVERED
THROUGHOUT BUCHAN • TOP QUALITY AND KEEN PRICES

...

DISPLENISH SALES BY PUBLIC ROUP BY ORDER OF THE EXECUTRY
OR SUBSCRIBERS AT THE HOUSE • AS ADVERTISED IN ADVANCE

...

PROPERTY SALES BY PUBLIC ROUP WITHIN THE PREMISES OR THE MART

...

AGENTS FOR CARTAGE FOR FISHCURERS DURING THE HERRING SEASON

...

TEA AND REFRESHMENTS SERVED AT THE BUFFET
HOT SOUP IF AVAILABLE

...

ADEQUATE PARKING FOR GIGS AND TRAPS ALONG THE CASTLE BRAES

...

TELEGRAPH BRODSEA NEAR FRASERBURGH

Alexander Bell

SECRETARY

On the return voyage from Yarmouth, steam drifters would call in at Blyth and fill their holds with coal. It cost only a pound for two tons of best. Alex Tait, who had the *Shepherd Lad*, took home a couple of tons for my father, and Wordie, the carter, delivered it to our door. Yarmouth shops opened very late at the end of the fishing. The boats would take home barrels of apples for everyone, and we took rock and chestnuts to roast on the bars of the grate. I had a few little nephews and nieces now, so I took home plenty.

The saga of the 'Turra Coo' was the news of the day. Most of the curers were death against compulsory national insurance payments, but John Ewen supported the idea. The whole thing was really causing quite a stir. At the same time the old age pension bill was passed, even though Lord Castlereagh and his supporters had fought against it all the way. He said working class folk had no right to such security! The pension started at five shillings a week for those over seventy and was a blessing to millions.

Before the First World War, the Broadsea Auction Mart was a busy place. They did not encourage droving cattle on the main road, so much of it was driven through Broadsea. They also had furniture roups. As bairns we liked to see all the beautiful things laid out. I remember my mother bought a table for an old sixpence. We still have it.

Chapter 8
'SUFFRAGETTES AND WAR'

It was Hogmanay night and all the young folk had gathered at the Broadgate. The pipe band was playing and I remember there was a crisp frost. 1914 came in with the peal of the Auld Kirk bells, the boys shaking hands with each other and kissing the girls. There was no booze. It was considered a disgrace for a young man to be the worse of drink. Everybody joined hands in enormous circles within circles and sang at the pitch of their voices:

"Take me back to the dear old Broch,
Castle Street and the auld kirk clock.
Tell them about the folk you meet,
Tell them to meet on Charlotte Street.
We will stop at the Saltoun Square,
All the youth of the Broch will be there
Here's tae yours and here's tae mine,
Gie us a kiss for a' lang syne!"

The last Bredsie walk took place next day. Of the huge crowd of young lads who met on the Broadgate that night, 500 were soon to lose their lives.

Kirsten and I were filleting with Davidson as the snow came and went again. At Easter we dyed Pess eggs for the bairns, an ancient custom. All the wifies gave the bairns a hard boiled egg, some painted with faces and bright colours. There were chocolate eggs, but they were never bought by ordinary folk.

You could go in at the back of 2 College Bounds and walk all the way to number 16. Horses and carts went through there. The ground was open between College Bounds and Noble Street - there were no dyked-in feus.

Kirsten Noble's family lived at 16 Noble Street before they moved to their new house. When Easter came, there was the usual activity of clanking bark pans and smoke from the fires at the west end of Broadsea as the fishermen barked their nets. The smell of the tar tubs was said to be healthy. The men used huge axes to break up the bark or tanning. Barratt houses now stand where the bark pans were.

The Aberdeen trawler *Drumoak* went aground at the Man's Haven, but was refloated at high water after her coal had been thrown overboard. The Customs officer did his nut! Before he could put a price on it, Bredsie wifies with creels and bairns with buckets and bags, gathered it up at breakneck speed! There were often shipwrecks at Rattray Briggs; it was a dangerous place. The St. Combs folk were said to have rugs and rolls of carpet up their but lums, hidden from the customs men who claimed everything from wrecked ships.

At the previous Yarmouth fishing a lot of German students had been working among samples of herring. They were quietly collecting information about the Yarmouth Roads, Scroby Island, Dudgeon, Newarp, Haseborough, Smiths Knoll and Corton, the names the fishermen used for the different sandbanks. The Peterhead fishing boat *Olive Branch* was lost with all hands at Corton.

The Irish girls arrived and we boarded the *St. Magnus*, once more bound for Shetland. It was a busy fishing. The Germans were buying and shipping the herring quicker than they were being branded! Instead of the murder of stacking full barrels three tiers high we were helping to row them on bogies to the Klondykers down at the wharf. We were filling up at four in the morning - the sun never set and the work never ended. I earned 12 sovereigns that summer, but it was hard graft. *HMS Ringdove* was back again, this time with a full complement of sailors.

The Shetland steamer 'St Magnus' leaving Fraserburgh.

As we papered the hut and posted our cards, we were
conscious of a sense of urgency in the air. I remember the
Suffragettes came to Balta looking for recruits. A wifie came
off the steamer and spoke to us on the pier. There were no
shop windows to smash there! She got a good clap but
returned as she came. On a Saturday night, a dozen or so
Swedish lads sat on herring barrels and played melodians
while we all danced. They did that every year. All the young
folk joined in, Dutchmen, Swedes, Royal Navy men and all
the young fishermen - even the German and Russian
Klondykers. It was an extremely pleasant atmosphere. Boy
Strachan from King Edward Street was my regular partner.
The Swedes showed us how to dance the 'Rylander' and we
taught them the 'Lancers' and 'Gay Gordons'. We all joined
together for the eightsome reels and danced till midnight!

It was June 1914 and once more great fleets of fishing
boats, yachts and cabin cruisers filled the sound. The travellers
who owned the luxurious craft made regular visits to Shetland
and often came ashore to watch us work. They were intrigued
by the speed we gutted herring. A liner full of rich folk

anchored in the loch for a few days; they were on a pleasure cruise. The night before they left Balta they had a grand deck party, with a proper orchestra. The strains of the beautiful music drifted over the loch as we worked. I heard a curer's son from Strichen Road tell his companion that he would have liked to have been out on the liner that evening. It was the same young man who later said, "Why do they allow that racket to carry on?" when we were dancing. The curers were in their own little class, stuck somewhere in the middle, jealous of upper class wealth and envious of working class comradeship and fun. They would have been welcome to join in with us, but convention didn't allow it. The dance on the liner went on until the small hours. It was June 1914 and, though we didn't know it then, the world was having its last great party.

A day or two later the Archduke of Austria was assassinated in Sarajevo and the German ships left the Shetlands in haste. In the mad rush, they took every herring, unbranded and all. Many curers were eventually made bankrupt by the Germans and Russians who never did settle their accounts for that year.

We waited anxiously for news as the papers came off the steamer. The fishing boats were advised to go home and the sailors on the *Ringdove* were given instructions to make ready for action. The steamship company asked the driftermen to take the coopers home with them to make room for the mass evacuation of the girls. Sottie's Andrew came round on the Friday morning shouting, "Come on you quinies, get packed up as quick as possible. There's going to be a War!"

The coopers left on the boats and we had to struggle with the heavy kists ourselves. We flung the bedding and everything over the stair in great haste, what a sad sight it was. We knew something terrible was about to happen. It was about six weeks before we got our kists and stock as most

of the Orkney and Shetland steamers were commandeered
by the Admiralty. Crammed aboard the *Earl of Zetland* we
all felt a great sense of relief as the ship cast off and slid past
Huney Island and into open water. We boarded the *St.
Rognvald* at Lerwick; the ship was absolutely jam packed. I
had never seen a ship so crowded; the water was well above
the Plimsoll line. Even the sheep and cattle pens were
occupied by girls! We sat high up beside the funnel. It was
warm there in the cold of the night. We sailed between the
land and the small island of Mousa where the ancient Pictish
Broch seemed to defy time itself. At the shore nearby, stood
a little housie with a jetty and a rowing boat at anchor. A
mannie and wifie waved to us from the doorway. I was
waving goodbye to Shetland forever.

We passed Sumburgh Head and nobody was sick!
Whether it was excitement or fear I couldn't say, but I
understood then how ordinary folk could perform
extraordinary deeds when the circumstances demanded. We
called briefly at Kirkwall and the Highland girls went ashore
at Scrabster. Ailey Davidson, a broch cooper, used to say that
if the Stornoway steamer *Sheila* went down there would be
nothing left floating but the quine's straw hats!

We thought of submarines as our ship ploughed through
the Moray Firth. Dozens of navy ships sailed close by us and
the sailors all waved and cheered. They were bound for
Invergordon and Scapa Flow. That was the last voyage we
made across the German Ocean. It became the North Sea
soon after that.

When the steamer berthed in the Broch on the Sunday
morning there was no-one at the harbour. The whole town
had gone to the railway station to wave the Territorials off
to war. Only about five of them came back. There must have
been two thousand Naval Reserves at the station. Many were
Highland men and there were others from the boats at
Sandhaven. They were leaving the Broch to join ships at

other ports, a sight that still lives clear in my memory.

That Sunday was such a sad day in the town. Opposite Dr Maconochie's house, on Commerce Street, Dickson had a three storey building which must have housed about a hundred herring workers. I saw a Highland girl clinging to her brother as he marched towards the station. She was in a terrible state at the parting and her tears flowed freely. Like the Territorials, few of the RNVR would see the Broch again and, of the Lewis men who did return, many were to perish on their own doorstep when the troopship *Iolaire* struck rocks as she entered Stornoway harbour in the early hours of New Year's Day, 1919. Their loved ones watched in horror from the quayside as the ship went down with more than two hundred men.

The Declaration of War was posted up on the Town Cross in Saltoun Square. Many thought it would be over by Christmas.

Gordon Highlanders on their way to Fraserburgh railway station,
5th August, 1914.

Gordon Highlanders at Barry Camp, 1914

The fishing ended there and then, and John Ewen paid us what we were due. As they nailed up the shutters on the fishworkers' huts, they were nailing the shutters on a golden age. My father, at the age of 56, joined the navy the following day with my brother Andrew. Two of my brothers joined the Naval Division and the other two, the Gordon Highlanders. Bill took pleurisy in the army barracks at Bedford and was discharged. He was at death's door for a long time.

A St. Combs man brought our china home from Baltasound on the *Milburn*. I remember the boat's number, FR 72, the same as our house. The skipper, I think, was Shoddie Love's father. We offered to spread his nets at Balta once but he wouldn't let us near them. "Awa ye go," he said, "if hens handle the nets there will nae be a hirrin' in them!" Like most fishermen, he was very superstitious. Though we were grateful to the man we wouldn't have cared if we had never seen the china again. We had much more important things to think about.

I got a job down in Lowestoft with Kirsten and Margaret, learning to kipper at Stirk's. We were living at Rant Score with Mrs Cafley - she was a kind landlady. We could no longer take a walk around the town at night; the shop windows were now in total darkness. Everything was blacked out. A wifie on the street shouted to us to take shelter as the "Zepps" were over. We didn't know what Zepps were, but we very soon found out! A pub called the 'Norfolk' at the end of the London Road was bombed and some civilian folk were killed. I suppose the Zeppelins were after the navy ships in the docks nearby.

Mrs Cafley, Christian's Lowestoft landlady.

Mary McLeod and two Broch sisters, Cis and Belle Simpson, were in the same digs and it was the first time that any of us had worked at the kippering. Though it was much cleaner than gutting, it was still cold work and our hands suffered just as badly. Kippers were split by hand then; there were no machines.

Stirk had a large fish-house that in peacetime employed a lot of women. The smoking kilns were in the middle with shutters on both sides and there was a fish-house on the ground floor with a packing loft above. Kippers were big business and had caught the London market. Our smoker was "Fussler Dinn" from Pitullie. He was shortly to leave for the forces.

Scena Scott was with us. She had a good sense of humour and, between her and "Fussler", we were always laughing. Smoking was very dangerous. Some of the kilns were very high and many a smoker slipped on the greasy slats and fell to his death.

We all went home for Hogmanay, but travelling was a nightmare in the blackout. There were constant air raid warnings as troop trains full of young lads passed us on their way south. After their six weeks training, my brothers had left with the Expeditionary Forces for France, leaving my mother alone at home. Our apprentice coopers, "Curly Crawford" and "Scrow Dingwell" joined the army. We had embroidered cards from both of them a few weeks before they died in the Flanders mud.

Bread and flour became very scarce in 1915 and pressure was put on the Government to control the production of drink. Lloyd George was very worried about feeding the nation and almost got the Government to pass total prohibition. Russia stopped making vodka and France cut down her wine output by two thirds, but that didn't affect any of us as we were strictly tee total. Rationing was enforced as food became more scarce. Each week we were allowed a half pound of sugar, 2 ounces of tea, 2 ounces of cheese, 5 ounces of butter or margarine, a shilling's worth of butchers' meat, a bar of washing soap and a bar of face soap. Folk were so undernourished it was no wonder that bad flu broke out at the end of the War. We had to work like slaves to achieve our victory, but I don't know how we managed on such meagre rations. It was the same again in World War II. Men were being called up from 16 to 60 unless they had key jobs. Many poor delicate laddies who were not fit for the army died in France. Medical boards passed almost anybody. It was shocking how Ministers of the Gospel urged 15 year old boys to go and fight. They should have gone themselves first!

"I wore a tunic, a bright khaki tunic,
And you wore civilian clothes,
You stole our wenches, while we were in the trenches,
Fighting the angry foes,
We fell at Loos, while you were on the booze,
Sleeping your sweet repose,
While I wore a tunic, a bright khaki tunic,
And you wore civilian clothes!"

'Keep the Home Fires Burning' and 'Pack up your Troubles' were the songs on everybody's lips.

When Jeannie, my brother John's wife, had a baby boy I stayed with her at 18½ Broadsea. They already had two little girls. We had intended to return to Lowestoft but had to register for work of national importance. Food production was in that class. The Broch Station's first class waiting room was used as a recruiting office, and it was there, next to a big bright coal fire, that Bengie's Kirsten and I were given the choice between work at the munitions factory or Keiller's foods in Dundee. We plumped for the latter. Kirsten had a winter jobbie with her former mistress, Mrs Reid the architect's wife. In the Buchan dialect the colour red is

pronounced "reed". Mrs Reid was furious when she learned
that Kirsten was leaving. "You selfish inconsiderate girl,
leaving me in the lurch with nobody to do my housework!"
It never struck her to do it herself. "Oh Mrs RED," said
Kirsten, "I am going to fight for my King and Country, I have
taken the King's shilling and now I must go!" The wifie was
not convinced. She was paying Chris a half-crown a week.

Doy Anderson at the Labour Exchange gave us chits
for our fare and we caught the Dundee train. A woman met
us at the Tay Bridge Station and helped us find digs. Dundee
was a completely new experience for the people of the North
East fishing and farming communities. The tenement housing
was terrible and bairns were still going to school on their
bare feet. There was an element of that in Peterhead and the
Broch, but in Dundee we saw a lot of bow legged
undernourished bairns on a scale that would match a television
documentary on Calcutta or Bombay. Many families lived
in just one or two rooms.

It was a busy city. The Tay was full of naval warships
and submarines, and there were hundreds of soldiers about
the place. The jute mills were working 24 hours a day making
sand bags for the trenches in France. The factory hooters -
the "bummers" - could be heard all over the city at five
o'clock in the morning. Mill owners were coining a fortune
from the war. For nearly a century, they kept the rotten
practice of employing women on pathetic wages as weavers
and spinners on the looms. In 1915, forty thousand women
were employed in the jute trade. It was common for mill
owners to employ loonies at the age of 14 and sack them
before they were 18 and entitled to a man's wage! The poor
boys were then shipped off to France with the Black Watch.
It was akin to fattening lambs for the slaughter. Sometimes
we sat in the old Howff to eat our supper. This ancient
graveyard was an old monastery garden, given to the city by
Queen Mary Stuart. The chaps from the Press and Journal

offices, which backed onto the cemetery, would often shout from the windows of their building and one of them used to sing:

> *"Wad ye come wi me tae bonnie Dundee,*
> *Whaur the jam and marmalade is made,*
> *Ye will see a lot o' funny sights,*
> *Ye never saw before, on the Esplanade."*

On Sunday nights we went to the mill girls' Gospel Meetings. The preacher there was known as "Blind Jeannie".

We went to work in our best coats and hats. Every employee had to appear as if they were going to the Kirk. Keiller's food canning factory was as clean as a hospital and we were given fresh overalls every day. Our nails had to be scrubbed in the washroom and our hair completely covered with a cap.

There were three grades: 'A' for Officers, 'B' for NCO's and 'C' for the common soldier. Everybody from the managing director to the 14 year old loonies who swept the floor were helpful and pleasant. Mary McLeod and Kirsten made Ceylon Toffees and Cis Simpson cut up ginger for chocolate gingers. That was grade A work. The B and C boys got boiled sweets. I sugared 'Ju-Jubes' till I was sick of the sight of them! We made 'Milky Tabs' and 'French Nougat Bars' and canned jam and marmalade. Grade A marmalade was thick cut and dark in colour. B and C were much the same, thin and watery. Signs were everywhere warning workers that they would be prosecuted if they stole or ate anything. There were no tea breaks. We worked from 7 o'clock till midday - then we were off to the washroom for a half bath. Lunch hour was from one till two, and we had another hour long break at 6 o'clock. For all the hours we worked we got 18 shillings a week. The wounded from Caird's Hospital were invited to dinner time concerts in the

Christian with her pal Christian Noble, "Bengie's Kirsten",
in their Keiller's uniforms.

Crystal Room and it was there that I first heard a girl sing 'When I come to the end of a perfect day'.

I had not been long in Dundee when a young soldier asked me where Dudhope Castle was. He had just arrived from Aldershot and was to be billeted at Dudhope, only a street away. We talked as we walked along and I told him I was on my way to work at Keiller's. When I came out of work two nights later, the laddie was standing at the gate. "I was looking for you," he said, "to ask if you would come to the pictures with me tomorrow."

I said yes, but I had no intention of going with him! When I told the others they said it would be rotten not a turn up, so I went. His name was Billy Wighton, a 19 year old Bannockburn coal miner who had worked in the pit since he was 14. We met almost every second night for the next six weeks. He was posted to France, but we wrote to each other regularly, and for the next three years Billy spent most of his leave time with me.

It was April 25th 1915 and we had been in Dundee for about three months. My mother was staying with my sister Jessie Anne in St. Monance. John and Peter had sailed with the troopship *River Clyde* to Gallipoli, so we advised mother to lock up 72 Broadsea and stay with Jessie Anne.

My brother John was killed at Cape Helles on 8th May 1915. He left a widow and three infants. Mother went home for a while but we told her to go back to Fife. She was in a dreadful state, and what comfort would she find sitting alone in a house of sorrow? On 25th July, Onty's Maggie Ann went to my sister-in-law, Mary Milne, and told her that a telegram boy had been at our house several times. The message was that my brother James had been mortally wounded on 15th July at Festubert, and had died three days later from a head wound. Alex Barclay from Broadsea was with him when he fell. The Padre wrote my mother a letter saying that, "James had found the Saviour".

AB John Dingwall Sim .

James Sim, seated, with John McAngus.

Chapter 9
'WILL THE CIRCLE BE UNBROKEN?'

My mother came home again from Fife, once more in a broken state. We were all stunned. Even after 60 years it's still painful. In the first week we tried to tell ourselves it wasn't true but, when a large parcel arrived from the military hospital in France where James had died, we were forced to accept the grim reality. My sister opened it and screamed at the pitch of her voice. It was the possessions of the late Private James Sim - a Gordon kilt and a tunic drenched in blood with two of my mother's letters in the pocket. My mother wanted to know why Margaret had screamed, but we never told her. I said it was the green coat she had sent to Perth to be dyed black, I showed my mother the coat which had arrived with the same post.

We dug a hole on the brae head under the clothes poles and, when our neighbour Gamrie Donald realised what we were doing, he dug it deeper for us. He was a kind man. We buried the kilt and tunic and most of the small trifles in the parcel. We kept James' watch, but hid it away from my mother. At least some of his blood had returned to his birth place.

There is a sequel to this. James had been on leave for a few days a fortnight before he was killed. I had travelled north with him from Dundee. The night before his leave was up, he was polishing his buttons at the fireside. I was sleeping in the kitchen box bed with my mother and Margaret, and James was in the but end. Mother said, "Look, he has fallen asleep by the fire." We all saw it, a soldier in a kilt, his head drooped. When Margaret rose to wake him there was nothing there. James was sound asleep in his bed!

We all left on the first train next morning and, when Margaret told James what we had seen the night before, he said, "You must have seen my ghost!"

Years later, a young barrister from Girvan came to Broadsea to buy a boat and stayed with us for a few days. He is now a Sheriff at Glasgow. I heard Margaret telling him about the apparition and that, if she regretted anything in her life, it was telling James what we had seen.

We were living in a daze. Every day we heard news of another sad loss. Margaret was exempted for a while to stay with mother but I had to go back to work. It was at about that time we got news of my cousin. He was serving with the Gordons in France and had been badly wounded. A bayonet had pierced his lung. He was brought back to Aberdeen but died in the Belmont Street School Military Hospital. His mother had no sons at home, so Margaret arranged the young man's funeral. The Commanding Officer said the military funeral could only take place to the station in Aberdeen. He is buried at the front of the dwelling house at Kirkton.

The Simpson girls went home to see their mother when their brother Henry was killed in France. Cis married a young soldier in Dundee and they both remained my friends for life. Seven of us had shared the same digs, but now only Margaret, Kirsten and I were at Keiller's. Lizzie Park went home to marry her soldier boyfriend, Mary McLeod married Alex Cowie, a romance that began at Baltasound, and Belle Simpson married George Phillip, an Australian who came over to join the navy. They settled at Timaroo in New Zealand.

We were lodging with Cis, now Mrs Taylor, and I had given her permission to open any telegrams that might come for Margaret or me. A telegram did arrive one morning, another real shocker. My brother Peter, who had gone all through the Dardanelles, had been killed at the Somme on November 13th 1916. His arm had been almost severed and was due to be amputated but Peter died on his way to the dressing station.

Four years later a small package arrived from the War Office. It was Peter's wallet. The army had been searching for bodies for re-burial and had found my brother. The note with it said that it had been "found on a fallen comrade". The wallet was mouldy and contained a letter from my sister and two photographs; one of little Margaret, our niece, and one of Albert Watt, a second cousin from New York who Peter had met up with abroad. They had been four years in the grave. My Granny Kirsty often wondered if my brother was the Unknown Warrior. For years they were lifting bodies from French farm land and burying them in official war graves. We found out later that Albert had been killed at Beaumont Hamel.

This killed my mother. She was 59 and suddenly looked as if she was pregnant. She became listless and not her usual cheerful self. She grew a strange yellow colour. The doctor said it was shock that started up the cancer. The pain she endured, with courage and dignity, for the next three months, I would not have wished on my worst enemy.

AB Peter Johnstone Sim.

Little Margaret, our niece
"To my uncle Pattie from your loving lassie Margaret Summers Sim. Hurry up and come home."

Sgt. Billy Wighton
"To my dear loving sweetheart".

Anne Taylor and James Sim, Christian's mother and father.

Once more, Margaret was given leave to stay with mother, but I was under conscription and had to return to Dundee. Only Billy Wighton's letters kept me going. He was wounded in December and was in hospital at Torquay. He had a bullet through his stomach and was quite ill to start with. We had been writing regularly and I had met his family by then. They were nice folk.

Billy, now Sgt. William Wighton, came north to meet my father and mother before he returned to France. My father was home for four days leave. They both liked the laddie - he was tee total and a non smoker - and were pleased to hear that Billy's folk were Methodist Chapel and had brought Billy up to be a good Christian. My parents gave their permission for our engagement, but told us not marry until the War was over. I remember my father's parting words to Billy, "Seek the Lord while he may be found, call upon him while he is near."

Billy and I explored the Bore Stone at Bannock Burn where King Robert raised his standard. In recent years I went on a bus run with the Broadsea Women's Guild to Stirling. The town now covers the open land Billy and I knew.

We got news that my mother was sinking fast, so Jessie Anne met me from Fife and we went home together. When Jessie Anne saw my mother she went into the lobby and broke her heart. We tried to keep it all from my Granny Kirsty, but she read the casualty lists every day in the Aberdeen Journal, lists that often filled a whole page. Two of Granny's great nephews were killed with the Anzacs at Gallipoli and another died at Beaumont Hamel (Peter had met both the Australian boys at Gallipoli. He had great admiration for the Australians. He said they were absolutely fearless and never took stupid orders from officers or anyone else). A fourth great nephew was one of the hundreds of souls lost when the *Lusitania* was torpedoed off the Irish coast. When my father tried to find out if the lad had been buried in Ireland, he was told that many of the recovered bodies could not be identified. Granny Kirsty corresponded with all those people.

My mother died in her bed in the corner of the kitchen at 72 Broadsea on February 1st 1917. I only wish I could have shared the terrible pain she suffered. My world fell apart that day. I loved her dearly. Miss Gladwell and the Salvation Army Captain said her funeral service and we sang, "Will the circle be unbroken." Miss Gladwell - I can hear her now - said, "Who are those arrayed in white raiment? It is they who have passed through great tribulations and washed their robes and made them white in the blood of the lamb."

My father came home in time to see my mother pass away, but had to leave on the first train after the funeral. Andrew was in Greece and couldn't get home. My father, my brother Bill and his son James (who was always my mother's favourite) and my sister's husband, Willie Innes, walked behind the hearse. I stood and watched as the sad procession left our house as so many had in generations past. I know that death is a fact of life, but in my own personal grief I found that hard to accept. First, there was my mother's bed in the corner. Then her coffin. And then there was nothing.

How strange and lonely our empty house was. It was like living through a terrible nightmare. As we spring cleaned the house we found so many memories of those who had gone. We gave the boys' clothes to the Salvation Army. Our faithful old aunt, Mary Jean, and her daughter Elizabeth Ann came to sleep in our house. Mary Jean's son Joseph had died of wounds and her other two sons were in the army. James, the eldest, was a cooper with Younger in Edinburgh before he left for France with the Royal Scots.

I had finished my term at Keiller's and was looking for another job at the fishing. Tom Jenkins, a Burghead curer, gave Kirsten and me jobs gutting and packing. He had taken over the Broch yard from Johnstone, the Yarmouth curer, whose daughter Amy was the famous pilot. There were a few Gamrie quines in the huts - Nellie Wiseman was one; she now lives in Cruden Bay. Jenkins' son was a nasty little snob! I remember the day he came up to me and said, "Who taught you to pack?" He sent the top tiers flying all over the ground. "Now pick them up," he shouted, "and start again!"

"Certainly not!" I replied, "You knocked them off, you pick them up!"

The foreman called me a cheeky beggar for speaking to the boss's son like that but, when I asked him if he could see anything wrong with my packing, he said, "No, nothing at all." The foreman picked up the herring for me. The curer's son was lucky I didn't smack him in the mouth!

I was living a half life. My heart was with Billy Wighton who was in the thick of the fighting in France, but still I was overcome with grief. Frances Duthie from Inverallochy was working with me and I was grateful for the kind encouraging words she gave me when I was feeling low. Frances was one of the best - she married in St. Combs but sadly died when she was still a young woman.

Before he left, Billy told me he would come to Broadsea and marry me as soon as the War was over. He said that he did not intend to go back to coalmining, but would take a chance at the fishing. He thought it couldn't be any more dangerous than mining miles under the ground with the roof ready to come down on you at any moment. The danger was what made so many miners Chapel people. The same could be said of the sea and fisher folk.

Billy told me more about mining than ever I had known: they told us nothing of that in school. A Scottish Act of Parliament permitted coal owners to keep colliers as slaves, with children under seven years of age working underground. Colliers guilty of disobedience to their masters were put in iron collars and in some places miners were not allowed burial in consecrated ground! The descendants were understandably bitter about their grandparents' servile lot. There were women and girls working in the mines and, even in the years before the First World War, conditions were far from satisfactory.

I got a job with Dickson at Yarmouth in September 1917. On the way south we saw a lot of Flying Corps boys at Maud Station, bound for the air-ship base at Lenabo. Two Broch lads had just come home from France and were washing Flanders' mud from their boots at the horse trough by the Station Hotel. One of them was Jimmy Sim. He married my friend Beatrice Noble. The other was John McAngus, whose sister had the Mallaig bakery.

Zeppelin raids continually disrupted our work at Yarmouth. When the warnings sounded, we made for the empty kilns. Billy Wighton got four days leave and when he came to see me, Mrs Sutton fixed him up with digs down the road. He wanted to stay in Yarmouth, but I told him he must go to see his family. Margaret and Kirsten agreed to let me off early so I could have dinner with Billy before he left. We had fish and chips in a cafe on King Street. I clearly remember waving goodbye to him at Vauxhall Station: he wrote often, sometimes twice a week.

We went back home to gut at the Castle Street yard. What a time that was. Every day we heard that some poor soul had been killed or wounded.

I have been to many weddings in my long life, including that of Princess Patricia's granddaughter, the Hon. Katherine Fraser, but none could compare with the one that took place in Broadsea on 19th September, 1918. Several folk have made mention of it. Mary Jane was a jovial character, short and absolutely round and, though folk tried to take the mickey, "she was all about." I can see her now going off to sell fish to cottars in the country. She rode high up on top of the baker's van with Willie McGregor, Craig the baker's van man, like a couple of Royal coachmen! Mary Jane was getting married to John Rollo, a son of Rollo the Broch mason.

Mary Jane's auntie Ellen, Jessie Tait, Margaret, Kirsten and I cleaned and papered her housie for the wedding. Her cousin, Jimmy Alex Crawford, was best man and his sister Nellie was bridesmaid. There must have been a thousand bairns beating biscuit tins; the noise was deafening! They formed a band and marched the couple to the dance in Broadsea Hall. It was packed with folk standing two deep on the windowsills and some had even climbed onto the entrance vestibule. My sister went round with a cap saying, "No change given," as a piper off a mine sweeper led the grand march. I recognised the piper. I'd seen him on the train at Inverkeithing. We danced till two in the morning and then went down to, "put the couple to bed". With the collection they were able to pay the band and give John and Mary Jane about £15.

Two days after the wedding, on September 21st, the boy I was engaged to was killed in France. Billy's sister Bella sent me a telegram immediately after his family had been

The Black Watch at Crieff Camp, Billy Wighton standing centre.

informed. I had just posted him a long letter telling him of all the wedding revelry. Ten days later my letter came back from the War Office stamped DECEASED.

On January 2nd 1918, we attended the wedding of Jemima Mearns and Bob McPhail, a cooper from Burghead. They had a big wedding in the Templar Hall and later emigrated to America like hundreds of others in search of a better life. My brother, Andrew, married Elizabeth Duthie from Rosehearty soon after that. It was very quiet. Two of Elizabeth's young nephews had been killed on January 10th when a mine drifted into the shore at Rosehearty. Seven people died and several more had been injured on that sad day. The boys were given snow to lick while the ambulance made its way through the drifts around the village. It did eventually arrive to take the injured to Maud, where a train had been arranged to take them into Aberdeen, but neither of Elizabeth's nephews survived the journey. The damage in the village was terrible. One house was completely demolished and the explosion rocked our house four miles away.

Shortly after that, another mine came ashore at the pebbly beach near the end of Broadsea, known to the older folk as Lady Urie's Shore. We were evacuated, but had nowhere to go. The war had taken everything from me - my three brothers, my mother and my boyfriend. I prayed to God that it would not take our home, humble though it was. Miller Ritchie gave us a hut in the big loft in Denmark Street and we slept the night on bare bed-boards with a quilt over us. The previous occupants had left a few lumps of coal, so we lit a fire and made some tea. Meg Lamb, who lived in Miller's house, kindly lent us two cups and some cutlery. She was very kind and told us to take what we needed. We put a luck penny in the little loonie's hand when we took her things back.

The Navy made the mine safe and I thanked the Almighty. The same thing happened in the Second World

WILL THE CIRCLE BE UNBROKEN'

War: a mine came ashore right under the houses at Broadsea. After it had been made safe, all the wifies joined in the "tug of war" to help the two Navy lads pull it up the brae. All the time an old mannie, "Epp's Tommy", was shouting, "Leave that alone, it will explode and kill ye!" They took the mine away on the back of a lorry.

In 1918, a trawler was firing at a fisherman's dan thinking it was the periscope of a submarine! The shells were exploding on the rocks at Broadsea. How they missed the houses I'll never know!

Dickson didn't go to Yarmouth in 1918. He was afraid to risk his employees' lives as the raids had been so frequent. Everybody was scunnered with the War. A whole generation of boys had perished and many had been so badly maimed they would never be able to work again. I had been Andrew's bridesmaid and Frank Burnett, on leave from the navy, was to have been his best man. Shortly before the ceremony, Frank received the terrible news that his brother had been killed in France. The Burnetts got what we got. Three of the brothers laid down their lives, all of them in their early twenties. Alex Crawford, whose brother George had been killed, stood in as best man. Alex had been badly wounded and would now have to manage on a pittance of a pension. The people used to sing:

"The moon shines bright on Charlie Chaplin,
His boots are cracklin' for the want o' blackenin'
And his baggy baggy troosers, we will mend them,
Before we send him to the Dardanelles!"

Georgie Buchan was only 14 when Bengie's Kirsten and I took him in hand at the fish-house. His mother, Jessie Ann Bogie, lived in Love Lane. She said he was slow to rise in the morning and told us to make sure he worked hard. I hadn't seen Georgie for 60 years until one day he called with his wife. They were on a visit from America.

In 1918, the steamer *St.Claire* was attacked by a submarine off the Fair Isle and two of the crew were killed. She returned fire and sank the submarine! Over the years we came to know most of the steamers' crewmen by sight.

I got a job kippering with Alex Lowe and was once more on my way to Yarmouth. There were about forty Broch women in the yard and some, whose husbands were in the forces, had taken their bairns with them. A serviceman's pay was so poor that women were glad to find a job. An ordinary soldier was paid a shilling a day. We went to work at the Denes in the blackout at five o'clock in the morning. Alex Lowe didn't allow us to take a single kipper, but we smuggled plenty to trade for tea and sugar at the barracks.

On our way to work on the morning of November 11th 1918, we met two naval ratings from *HMS Electra*. They told us that an armistice was to start at eleven o'clock that day! We were busy packing kippers when a policeman called at the yard to tell us there would be a two minute silence at eleven o'clock and to watch out for the maroons.

The herring came in and we started to split them. Everyone was tense. We could hardly believe the War was nearly over. The maroons went off and we laid down our knives for the two minute silence. A vast crowd had assembled along the Marine Parade but our boss, who had danced the height of himself as the rockets exploded, told us to get on with our work. "There's no need for that nonsense,"he said, "I want these herring split and ready for the smoker!"

Most of us ignored the man. We threw off our aprons and made for the town. The ships in the river were all blowing their hooters and we could hear church bells ringing in every direction. 'Very' lights shot into the sky as shells from the ships' guns burst high out over the sea. A great parade made its way through the town - at least thirty thousand troops and naval units, all with their bayonets fixed. Drums rolled as officers on horseback led the procession up the Regent Road and on to King Street. Hundreds of maimed servicemen, most of them from the Melton Lodge Hospital, were being pushed along in bath chairs by Boy Scouts. It was one of the saddest sights I have ever witnessed. Some of them were blind, others had lost limbs or were in some way horribly disfigured. Mustard gas had given many of them a queer jaundiced look. I wondered how these poor souls would fair in our "land fit for heroes!" I was thankful that my own loved ones had at least been spared that humiliation.

The Lord Mayor took the salute from the Town Hall balcony as the Yarmouth flag was hoisted on the steeple. Alderman Harbord actually wept as he announced the number of Yarmouth and Gorleston boys who had laid down their lives. The crowds on the Hall Quay heard him say that those who had lost dear ones should rejoice in the knowledge that such losses would never have to be suffered again!

Alex Lowe gave the few blacklegs who had stayed on at work a lousy five shillings. My sister Margaret, well known for her fiery temper, went at Lowe like no man's business. "You dirty rotten pig! You wouldn't honour those who gave their lives for you! You bloomin' shirker! You got your kippering yard so you could dodge the War and you, a young able bodied man, living in grand hotels while others were dying in the trenches!"

The Wick women joined in with a barrage of insults. They too had lost husbands and brothers. I really think Lowe was disappointed to hear the War was over, for it meant an end to his government contract and the fortune he was raking in ended with it.

It was a great relief to know that the War was at last over, but what a world to wake up in. The people realised they had been conned and the blame fell on the shoulders of

Haig, Churchill and Kitchener. Everybody was screaming for the Kaiser to be hanged, but of course he wasn't. Many folk thought our armies should march on into Berlin and take over, and that if they didn't we might all be at war again in no time. How right they were!

Local boys married English girls, kitchen maids married officers and the whole set up was strewn with broken marriages. There were strikes and lockouts everywhere, things unheard of before, and mass pay cuts led to total chaos among the workers. When the navy cut the ratings' pay, but left the officers' pay intact, mutiny broke out at Invergordon. It was the opposite of a country fit for heroes. The ruling class stupidly thought that all would return to normal over night. Millions on both sides had lost their lives believing they were fighting a just cause. We all believed the false promises that the politicians doled out, but by the 1930s people were actually starving! Miners' bands were going around the towns glad of any coppers the public might throw to them.

Shortly after my mother died, Beatrice Maconochie, a colonel's daughter who married the Rev. Finlayson of Lonmay, became president of the North East Government Charity Fund. She told us our case had been assesed and offered us £5. They had carried out their investigation without our authority and Margaret went wild. "Though you had offered us five hundred pounds," she said, "we would never have accepted it!" What a cheek to think that that was what my brothers' lives were worth.

We broke our journey south that year at Edinburgh and stayed with our cousin's wife Kate from Seisadar on Lewis. She had a beautiful house in Spence Street, Newington. University students boarded there. Kate's sister, Bella, arrived from Stornoway while we were there. We met her at Waverley Station and Margaret helped carry her bags. They were heavy with chickens and all sorts of things that we found hard to get on the mainland. She had half a pig in one case! Kirsten and I followed while Kate and Bella were busy in the Gaelic.

Sometimes we broke the journey with a visit to Jeannie Ireland, another cousin, in Burntisland. She was a likable warrior with real Buchan character. Nobody ever got the better of Jeannie!

Bill Noble came home from the war a hero. He was awarded the DSM for the part he played as a crewman on the drifter *Gowanlea*. Many said he should have got the VC. Bill married Jeannie Wilson at Broadsea Hall. Jeannie worked for Dickson's and a whole lot of us young folk went to the wedding. The couple were to set up their new home in College Bounds, next to Broadsea Farm - the classy part of Broadsea. Kirsten and I left the dance and sneaked round to the house. Nobody locked their doors in those days. We went in quietly, undid the window latches and then made our way back to the Hall. The couple left for home at about midnight and a whole gang of us followed them up the road. We let them settle before we climbed through the windows. Bill was sitting at a bonnie fire and Jeannie was making a cup of tea. What a surprise they got when we all walked in! We were there until about four in the morning. What fun and laughter! It was common practice to "bed" a newly wedded couple then, if you could get away with it, but they were usually fly and took steps to prevent it happening. Bill and Jeannie eventually went to live with her folk at 80 Broadsea, two doors from me. We shared each other's joy and sadness. They lost their son when he was four and their married daughter died quite recently.

One of the Broadsea shoppies was kept by William Noble, "Wulla Boodie", and his wife Jean McNab. They were childhood sweethearts, but didn't marry until they were both about sixty! The entrance to their shop was a little door at the back. At that time it looked out over open fields as far as Mormond Hill. Jean made a good living selling haberdashery. Folk made all their own clothes then so there was a good market for all that stuff. I can remember buying paraffin from old blind Jimmy along the road at number 67.

Churchill wanted to continue the War and put down the Bolsheviks. British troops had invaded Russia, but the dockers were refusing to load supply ships. The majority had agreed that enough was enough. The flowers of our nation had been slaughtered, and what for? The War to end all war had turned out to be a complete flop. None of the Government's promises were ever honoured and the demobbed servicemen were sold down the river.

Chapter 10
'A COUNTRY FIT FOR HEROES!'

Most of the curers who started up again after the war were using motor lorries in preference to horse drawn carts. Margaret, Kirsten and I were now working with Alex Gordon in Castle Street and Jimmy Sim was his lorry driver. A couple of years before that, we were passing through Maud on our way home from the Yarmouth fishing when we met up with Jimmy and a few young Gordons just home from the Front. I remember we treated them all to tea at the Station Hotel. They later sent us postcards from France. The lorries did a fine job, but we missed the cheery chatter and songs of the country horsemen:

> "Some ran on horseback, ithers ran on fit,
> but the puir auld wifie quidna sit,
> She clawed the steel, instead o' her hip,
> and aye she cursed and banned!"

With most of the young men lying in unknown graves, tradesman were very hard to find in 1919. Old coopers were brought out of retirement to teach their skills to apprentices. Some were eighty years old, and very grumpy! It was extremely hard work and the pay then was only 28 shillings a week. During the fishing they often worked an 18 hour day.

When a mass demonstration came into conflict with the police in Glasgow's George Square, they cleared the rioters with a baton charge and over a hundred people were seriously injured. Coalminers resented the wage cuts private mine owners had brought in and their protests resulted in mass lockouts. It was doubtful if there would be enough coal available to drive our special trains down to East Anglia. The

Government had not accepted the recommendation by the Royal Commission to nationalise the coal mines. The mine owners won the day and the result was widespread unemployment and unrest.

Winston Churchill said Glasgow looked like Moscow. He sent the troops in, supported by tanks and navy ships to quell the 'Red Clyde Revolutionaries'. We didn't think it concerned us in the fish trade, but the railwaymen planned to strike in sympathy with the miners. They too had suffered crippling pay cuts.

Our train left Fraserburgh for Yarmouth on Friday September 30th and, when we went into Aberdeen for an hour, we found many of the shops closed and shuttered for fear of rioting. The atmosphere was really tense. Police were everywhere and soldiers patrolled the city. A whole regiment was put on stand-by at the Castlehill Barracks. We left Aberdeen coupled to the Peterhead special, but had only travelled as far as Montrose when news broke that the railwaymen were going on strike at midnight. An old engine driver took us down to Dundee and then on to Edinburgh. The Princess Street gates were locked up, so there was no trouble at Waverley station. We pressed on to Berwick-on-Tweed but that was as far as we got that night. The line was blocked with sticks and stones and a pile of old iron bed ends. We were in a real dilemma. Few of the married women with bairns had any money. They were put up in church halls and other public places. I found digs in Church Street with Margaret and Kirsten.

We were terrified of the strikers. Huge stones rattled on the train roof and many windows were broken. Soldiers with fixed bayonets guarded the station. We had to report there every day so we asked a policeman to accompany us. They were decent lads. They even gave us tea in the waiting room. The Mayor and Mayoress of Berwick invited us all to supper in the Town Hall. It was packed to overflowing and they certainly did us proud! Smoker's Mary Annie from Buchanhaven stood up and said grace before we tucked into hot mince pies and home bakes. I saw a wifie stuffing all she could into her patent leather bag! We were in Berwick for nearly a week and Kirsten and I explored the whole place. I remember visiting the ramparts of the ancient city walls. They must have seen some changes.

Some North East boats came in and gave us supper. Willie Watt of the *Solace* gave a crowd of us a meal, and so did the Cairnbulg boat *Sunshine*. She was owned by the May family, my mother's distant relations.

In the middle of the night, the police took us across to Tweedmouth and down a lonely tree-lined lane to the station. What an experience! We wished we had stayed at Montrose. Soldiers took over the train and, with a clank and a shudder, we were on our way again. The pickets at Newcastle were violent. Even at that hour, the blinds had to be pulled down and our luggage piled high against the windows and doors. Stones crashed onto the roof and the sound of breaking glass came from all directions. York and Peterborough were even worse. The little bairns were put under the seats. Some of the older ones appeared to be enjoying the experience and had to be kept out of the corridors and away from the windows. If anyone had put their head out they would have been killed!

We were held up again in Kings Lynn and this time the train was so badly damaged it was a miracle that nobody was seriously hurt. There was nowhere to hide. In the crowded station booking hall an elderly well-dressed man prayed that we would have a safe journey to Yarmouth. He asked us to raise our voices and sing, "The Lord is My Shepherd". After that we sang, "Oh for a thousand tongues to sing my great Redeemer's praise". The whole station rang with song!

Somebody suggested fish and chips, so Kirsten and I volunteered to go with a couple of girls from other coaches.

We climbed the barbed wire fence and a mannie told us where the nearest chip shop was. What a nice woman the chip shop wifie was. She gave us all a cup of tea while she fried a hundred weight of chips. My did we enjoy it! "Watch yourselves darlings," she said, " the pickets here are hostile!"

When we got back to the fence, the police were about to arrest us, but our accents were proof enough of who we were. They held the huge parcels of chips while we climbed back over. That fish supper was the most welcome I ever had. We reached the now familiar Vauxhall Station in a hail of stones and abuse. The war was over and never before had the working classes been more firmly united against the ugliness of the class system.

In the Broch, the North School had provided a steady supply of coopers, fishermen and gutters and packers. That was our calling and we had accepted our lot without question. Now it would be different. A million had died for better conditions, but where were they?

Employers thought that by cutting back wages they could win back the pre-war markets. Much of the trouble today lies at the door of those people. Lloyd George's Coalition was defeated in 1921 and a Tory Government came to power the following year. It was England that put them in. They really had no mandate to govern Scotland. Labour had the most seats, but Bonar Law continued to force English dominance on the Scottish people causing a great deal of resentment north of the border.

We were back with Mrs Sutton in the Rows. It was a cold damp winter, with showers of wet sleet that seemed to cut right into our bones. I had a bad cough all the time I was there, so I was glad when the fishing was over and we were on our way back home.

For the last year of the War, my father had been the harbour master at Peterhead. He stayed with the Cowie Reids, Salvation Army folk who remained our good friends.

After the War he got the job of berthing master at Fraserburgh. He had seen a lot of active service and was not the same man: the War had made him more tolerant of folk. Robert Duthie told me of an incident at sea when my father saw a Broadsea man get his head blown off. The poor man's family had thankfully been spared the gruesome details.

The *Venture* had lain derelict for all the War years, though we did give her a clean up from time to time, and had always paid her dues. The sleeping accommodation was aft, but now they were converting her to steam the sleeping berths would have to be moved forrit. The expense of conversion was out of the question, so my father sold the boat to Jimmicky Lobban in Rosehearty. He was a near cousin of both my mother and father: in North East Scotland we only had to scratch the surface to see how inbred we were.

My father was with the Navy until 1920, taking drifters with a four man crew down to Portland and Milfordhaven. For a couple of years, several minesweepers were stationed in the Broch. A cousin of ours, Finlay McKay, was aboard the *Orphens*; he came from Port Skerra in Sutherland. When my father was on nightshift at the Broch harbour, I would take his tea down to the old watchman's hut for him. Often old Jakie Carle and Lord Saltoun (he was living at Witch Hill then) would be sitting with my father. I always took enough for three.

One wild night, a lot of trawlers were forced into the harbour. A trawlermen, who was a stranger to us all, came into the hut and grabbed my father by the throat. Our Spaniel doggie would have torn him to pieces! He thought my father collected the harbour dues and demanded he hand the money over! Captain Stephen, the Harbour Master, reported him to the police and the offender was duly arrested and given three months in jail. My father was badly shaken by it all.

The night after the hold up, he was loosing the ropes

of the new steam ship *Corby Hill* when he overbalanced and fell into the icy water. Jimmy Sim, "Jimmy Da", a local lifeboat hero, rescued my father from the dock, but he became seriously ill with pleurisy soon afterwards and never worked again.

Not long after that, I was on my way home from a wedding, a quiet affair at Mrs Hepburn's house on High Street. I was alone. There were no longer any escorts - all the young men had been wiped out. It was at that time that we started to see girls dancing with each other. I was almost at my door when a man attacked me and knocked me to the ground. I screamed and my father came out of the house and ran after him but he got away. The matter was reported to the police, but nothing ever came of it. I recognised the man years later and he pulled his cap down over his eyes. I told him what I thought of him and he beat another hasty retreat. It was a fearful experience.

I went to Yarmouth with Alex Gordon in 1920, another cold wet winter. We were constantly soaked on the freezing Denes. Mrs Sutton tried everything to shift my heavy cold but it lingered on and on until I eventually contracted tuberculosis. That was to be my last season at Yarmouth and I didn't see the place again until my daughter and her husband took me there fifty years later. What a change! Like Peterhead and Fraserburgh, it got a terrible battering in the Second World War and the Rows had been razed to the ground.

After a brief spell at home, I was sent to the sanatorium at Bridge of Weir, near the Quarrier's Home for orphan children. Though I was sick, I was grateful when I saw those poor bairns, and thanked God for the mother He gave me for those short twenty years. Death's rolling tide had carried my loved ones away. My brother John was 26, James 24, Peter 20 and Billy Wighton was 22. They remain those ages in my memory. They never grow older.

The flu epidemic that followed the War killed more than the holocaust had done. Whole families were wiped out. I don't think they ever really knew what kind of virus had caused it. A person would be hale and hearty one day and stretched out on a table the next. The War killed a million and the flu killed a million and a quarter. I always thought it might have been a touch of that flu that started my tuberculosis.

Christmas came but the festive spirit was hard to find. I remembered "Black Peter", a young Dutchman we met at the Shetland fishing. He used to push bogies of herring from the Dutch boats up to the yards. We wondered how he got that name - he was a tall blonde man - but we later learned that "Black Peter" is Santa Claus' assistant in Holland.

I had the fresh air treatment at Bridge of Weir. All the windows were kept wide open all night. They moved me to Insch Hospital for a while after that. When I came home, I wasn't prepared for the dreadful experience of being shunned in the street. People would cover their mouths when they saw me and walk away. The TB bugs couldn't compete with the boisterous Bredsie breezes and, with God's help, I soon started to feel better. Bella Watt, Jimmy Findlay's wife, told me never to lose heart. She always found time to speak to me. Old Liza's Jeanicky lived at 34 Broadsea. She was a kind old soul who had given a home to several orphan bairns. She told me to hold my head high and face those who shunned me with dignity. After Jeanicky McLeman's son Willie had enlisted in the Navy she was alone in the house. Bengie's Kirsten was Jeanicky's granddaughter, and Kirsten and I used to sleep sometimes in her but end to keep her company. She sang to us all the old songs. I wish I could remember them.

Jeanicky's cottage was in the middle of a terrace with the doors facing the sea. One morning we were just up when an awful rapping got up on the back window. It was

McRobbie, our short-sighted ill-natured postie. "McLeman, thirty four," he shouted, "where the hell's your door?" Jeanicky yelled back at the top of her voice, "Ye impudent brute, gang roon the corner and look for it, ye will hae ma windie cad in!"

With TB, most people had a slow lingering death. I had made my peace with God, and would accept it if it came. My father put another storey on our house and it was thoroughly modernised with proper sanitation. While this was being done, we were still living in the house, though much of our stuff was stored with my sister Jessie next door. A deafening clumping noise came from above one day and we rushed out to see what was happening. A crowd of young folk from Dickson's had gathered on the corner and a Broch loon, Alex Pirie, had taken a horse from the Waul Park and led it up the mason's ramp onto the roof of our house! My father took it all in good part.

It was with a heavy heart that I saw all my friends off to Yarmouth that year. My father told me if I ever went back to the fishing I would land in the Kirkton Churchyard! Out of the goodness of her heart Mrs Hepburn gave me a job in her boarding house by the 'Picture House' in the High Street.

When Spring arrived, Alex Gordon asked me if I would like to help clean their house in Grattan Place. 'Seafield' was a very beautiful house. The Gordons only used it in the summer months when their children came up from Aberdeen for a holiday. Their housekeeper came through from their enormous mansion in Aberdeen's Queen's Road. The pay was only four shillings a week. But I was grateful from the depth of my heart to be well again and able to work, even if many folk still gave me a wide berth for dread of consumption.

An apprentice joiner rang the Gordon's front door bell at 8 o'clock one morning and I let him in. He was to take down all the roller blinds and I was to wash the windows and the net screens. Every window on the front of the house had a beautiful leaded glass screen and on the central panel of each one there was painted scenes from the herring harvest. They had been done by a local artist, Webster, and I'm sure would be very valuable today. Though the joiner laddie worked steady, the housekeeper only brought tea through for me. There was only the housekeeper and me there, and she had already choked me off for letting the boy in through the front door. I said, "What about a cup for the boy?" I got an icy stare, but she did relent and brought another cup. She later explained to me that, "It simply isn't done in good houses." I asked her what so many had fought and died for. Was it to continue this stupid carry on?

About a month after the Armistice, the Fraserburgh lifeboat, *The Lady Rothes*, turned over and several of the crew were drowned. Navy ships were still in the harbour and their crews, in white caps and gaiters, attended the funeral. It was a moving sight. I was to see another two life boat disasters in Fraserburgh. *The John and Charles Kennedy* capsized near the harbour in February 1953 and *The Duchess of Kent* was lost in January 1970. Many lives were lost, but that's what people who make a living from the sea constantly have to endure. Our utmost efforts surely fail to comprehend God's love.

When the slaughterhouse was moved from Broadsea to the reclaimed ground at the harbour, those who witnessed the swarms of rats flitting from their old home to their new one said it was quite terrifying! The rats were everywhere running down the High Street and into Cross Street in one great seething mass!

Margaret, Kirsten and Mary Hepburn were now crewed together at Dickson's. There were five selections to make - large full (mature herring containing milt or roe), full, large spent (herrings that have shot their roes), mattie full and matties (gutted herrings over nine inches long) - and only by the gutters' skill did the herring find the right tub.

Like everybody else, the herring girls were paid pre-War wages which was not enough to live on. Nellie May from Inverallochy, known as "Nell Gray", was spokeswoman for Dickson's quines when they went on strike. It was the first in the history of the Broch fishing. A crew was paid tenpence a barrel, that's less than 2p today, and fourpence an hour for filling up. For a 14 hour day of punishing labour the girls got about 11p! Young folk today can't believe we worked for that kind of money. Nellie told Alex Gordon, Dickson's adopted son, that they wanted a shilling a barrel for gutting and tenpence an hour for filling up. He said, "Go back to work girls, I'll get it all fixed up!".

My sister Jessie Anne had a late child which I took for long walks in a shawl. I was very fond of the little lad. His brother somehow always seemed to fall out with the others and always came to me for consolation. They're nearly all in New Zealand now, but we still keep in touch.

In spite of my illness I have outlived all my family. I'm the last of Bouff's Jimmy's 42 grandchildren. I now live at 84 Broadsea, one of the oldest houses in the village and the happiest I have ever lived in. Here I have found peace of mind in my old age. I married Douglas Marshall in 1922 and we had two sons and two daughters. I have had nine grandchildren - one died in infancy - and I am also a great grandmother. My sons are both on the sea.

The 1930s saw the worst slump yet. When my father was dying, he told us not to mourn. "I am going to a far better place," he said. He spoke of all the poor souls who had gone before him, including Billy Wighton the lad I said goodbye to at Vauxhall Station in Yarmouth. I remember Billy had left his new sergeant's swagger cane on Mrs Sutton's kitchen table. He realised what he had done as his train pulled away. I offered to post it, but he said he would get another in Edinburgh. He told me to keep it - it's still in the house yet.

Christian and Douglas Marshall, 1922.

Just before my father passed away he said, "My Saviour's precious blood has made my title sure."

Andrew and Elizabeth emigrated to America with their family. People poured over the Atlantic in search of work. Some had a tough time in the States but things were no better here. It's as clear as daylight, if Maggie Thatcher has her way those days will return!

We were living at 72 Broadsea and my eldest son was a schoolboy. I gave him a piece and jam and he bit out the centre and threw the crusts away. A clean and tidy looking man was sitting on a seat looking out across the sea. He didn't know I could see him from my gable window, and he grabbed the crusts my son had flung away and quickly ate them. I gave the man tea and something to eat. He said he hadn't eaten since the previous day. He was a cooper from Edinburgh and had been on foot to the whisky country at Speyside to look for work. We didn't have much in those days but I offered him some money. He wouldn't take it. That was our country fit for heroes!

We started to cure and dry haddock and cod for Miller Ritchie. My brother-in-law, Willie Innes, was in charge and we employed our neighbours James Crawford and his daughter Maggie. Tons of fish went through our hands.

When Lord Saltoun's daughter, the present Lady Saltoun, married Captain Alexander Ramsay of Mar, a great stir was caused in the Broch when it became known that Queen Elizabeth, the Queen Mother, and Queen Ingrid of Denmark were to be guests. Some years later, when Lady Saltoun's daughter, Katherine, married Captain Mark Nicolson, my son and I were invited to their wedding in the Episcopal Kirk in the Broch. It was a colourful affair. I remember when I stumbled on the aisle carpet an immaculately dressed lady took my arm to prevent me from falling and led me up the aisle and out the door. She spoke pleasantly all the time. She was Her Royal Highness Princess Margaret of Yugoslavia. The reception at Cairnbulg Castle was very pleasant. General Sir David Fraser called over all the Saltoun offspring and introduced me as his kinswoman. In the past, we would have gone to great lengths to hide that kind of thing.

Now in my late eighties I remember when I was once a part of a great empire. In the earlier part of my life, no-one could have dreamt that fishermen and bakers' and butchers' loons would be called to take part in the carnage of two World Wars! Ours has been a bloody century, and it's not over yet. The other day, a sailor from Broadsea called to see me with his young wife. He had recently returned from the Falklands War. In my lifetime I have seen Great Britain reduced to a third rate country, but still we are told that the State knows what's best for us. All that we worked for, and so many died for - the welfare state - will be back to square one if the Tories have their way!

The wedding of The Lady Saltoun of Abernethy and Capt. Alexander Ramsay of Mar, 1956.

The wedding of The Hon. Katherine Fraser and Capt. Mark Nicolson, 1980.

I thank God every morning and night for all the blessings I have. My granddaughters, Patricia and Anne, are very kind to me and look after me well. Every night without fail their yellow mongrel doggie comes to see me. It gets up on a stool and rattles the handle of my dresser for a couple of Polo mints. A greedy seagull also comes to see me, and a one legged crow! I feed them both at the door every day.

How quickly our lives fly away. I often wondered what Alexander Fraser would have thought if he could have looked down from the ramparts of the castle he built at Kinnaird 400 years ago to see the vast curing stations invading the farm land right to his door. Many of the quinies working in the yards were his very own descendants. I think of the responsibilities and problems inheritance creates. Now I am the owner of 72 Broadsea, but only a link in the chain. It is presently let to oil people and it seems strange to see a three year old Texan quinie looking through the gable window as my children and grandchildren did, and so too did my Granny Kirsty when she was young, and other bairns as far back as the days of Sir Alexander the founder. Life is so short.

Family portrait photographed on the eve of Andrew's departure for the United States, 1927.

Christian   Andrew   Margaret
James Sim   Jessie Anne   Bill

My other grandchildren are scattered. I don't see them often, but think of them always. The other day Peter Malcolm, a nice laddie, came to see me. He is going to the South Pole with Robert Swan, to follow in the footsteps of Captain Scott. My son James helped them find a suitable ship for their expedition which will soon be leaving Fraserburgh harbour. When we hear so much of drink and drugs it's good to see young laddies attempt such a thing today.

Robert Swan: the first man to walk to both North and South Poles, visiting Broadsea on his return from Antarctica.

I have seen two terrible World Wars. Will man never learn to live at peace? The older I get the less I see the reason for killing each other. To look back on nearly 90 years, yesterday is only a dream. Tomorrow is a vision of hope.

Today, change is so rapid.
Everything changes but God.

GLOSSARY

bann:	swear, curse
bark:	a preserving solution for nets
bauchles:	worn out shoes
bigsy:	conceited, snooty
bellman:	town crier
chiel:	chap, fellow
conversache:	social gathering
cran:	measure of herring, four baskets or one fifth ton
creel:	basket
dan:	marker buoy
dallies:	dahlias
dinned:	forced, thumped
farlanes:	long wooden troughs
ferlies:	strange happenings
forrit:	forward part of boat
fussler:	whistler
girnal:	oatmeal barrel
girny:	cantankerous
gollachy:	earwig (gollach) ridden
Govey Dicks!:	a cry of surprise
kwites:	oilskin skirts
loon, loonie:	lad, little boy
mutch:	bonnet, cap
quine, quinie:	girl, little girl
reddin':	unravelling, tidying up
reek:	smoke
roosin' tubs:	wooden salting tubs
scaups:	mussel beds
scunnered:	fed up
sheeled:	shoveled or shelled
skirlin':	shrieking
spoot-holes:	holes in curing yard walls
throwither:	very untidy
tirred:	stripped
trig:	smart
Wasten:	west end of village
windie cad in:	window knocked in, broken